Gun Carry In The USA
Your Right to Self-defense

LEGAL DISCLAIMER
The information presented in this book is not intended as a complete course in gun safety and is not a substitute for formal qualified instruction in the handling, use, or storage of firearms.

MAINE-PATRIOT.com
3 Linnell Circle
Brunswick, Maine 04011

maine-patriot.com

Gun Carry In the USA

The right to self-protection is not a political privilege but one of the inalienable rights in the Declaration of Independence; the right to life granted by God.

Gun Carry In the USA

A right unexercised is a right lost.

Gun Carry In Maine

Contents

Your Right to Self-defense

THIS BOOK is dedicated to the former President of the MONMOUTH FISH AND GAME ASSOCIATION

NRA Instructor
John R. Valonis
of Monmouth, Maine

who taught the author to **"ALWAYS keep your finger OFF the trigger until ready to shoot!"** — And disciplined him — and scolded him — to *never forget* this; the *most important* of all Gun Safety Rules.

Discipline = Love

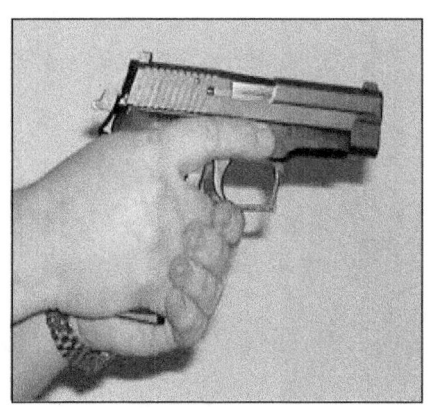

BASIC GUN SAFETY RULES

1. ALWAYS keep the gun pointed in a safe direction!

2. ALWAYS keep your finger OFF the trigger until ready to shoot!

3. ALWAYS keep the gun unloaded until ready to use!

Gun Carry In the USA

Introduction

During the 2008 campaign in America, then presidential candidate Barack Obama made a startling statement revealing his desire to implement a program involving ordinary citizens like you and me **as 'snitches'** who feel empowered like they are part of the Department of Homeland Security, the FBI, or another law enforcement agency.

Obama openly stated, *"We cannot continue to rely only on our military in order to achieve the national security objectives that we've set. We've got to have a civilian national security force that's just as powerful, just as strong, just as well-funded."*

Better to **carry concealed** — than to **be 'snitches'** on our neighbors and friends.

The Department of Homeland Security launched a program where they decided to "partner" with Boy Scouts to **"prepare youth for more traditional jobs as police officers and fire fighters."** And the New York Times ran an article in 2009 discussing a drill involving young boys and girls where they used fake rifles and were trained to confront a **"disgruntled Iraq War veteran"** who had become a domestic terrorist.

Boy Scouts or Hitler's Youth — you decide

Scouts Train to Fight Terrorists, and More

IMPERIAL, Calif. — In a training exercise run by Border Patrol agents, Explorer scouts from Visalia, Calif., prepare to storm a "hijacked" bus.

The responding officers — eight teenage boys and girls, the youngest 14 — face tripwire, a thin cloud of poisonous gas and loud shots - **BAM! BAM!** - fired from behind a flimsy wall. They move quickly, pellet guns drawn and masks affixed.

"United States Border Patrol! Put your hands up!" screams one in a voice cracking with adolescent determination as the suspect is subdued.

It is all quite a step up away from the square knot.

Gun Carry In the USA

TOP 10

REASONS TO
CARRY CONCEALED

1. **Safety:** this may seem like a no-brainer, but really, there seems to be a growing need to protect oneself and one's family.

2. **Ease of obtaining a permit:** People in the state may not realize how easy it is to obtain your **Concealed Carry Permit**. As long as you meet the general requirements, it is rather inexpensive to obtain the permit.

3. **To improve gun safety:** Part of becoming a concealed carry permit holder means that you have attended at least a basic course of instruction on how to handle firearms safely (there are so many people who are misinformed about guns because of Hollywood movies).

4. **Increase gun knowledge:** By regularly carrying concealed, and handling firearms, your knowledge about firearms will increase (i.e. do you know the difference between single-action, double action, adjustable or fixed sights, etc?).

5. **Be an example:** By carrying a concealed weapon, it's inevitable that someone will see your gun one

day and ask you why you carry. You'll probably respond that you carry because it's your second amendment right to, or because you want to remain safe.

6. **Exercise a Constitutional right:** The U.S. Supreme Court just recently reaffirmed what most American's already knew; that the right to bear arms isn't just about being a part of a militia. You have the constitutional right to keep and bear arms.

7. **For convenience:** Now it might sound silly to say that having a **Concealed Carry permit** is convenient, but think about it for just a second. If you don't have a concealed carry permit it is against the Law to travel with loaded gun(s) in your vehicle.

8. **Being a good citizen:** Carrying a concealed gun means that you are committed to being an active participant in society. It means this because you have to know the law, be involved in the law, and take steps to fulfill the law. Do you realize how unique that is? How many people have you come into contact with who are completely ignorant of what the law is?

9. **Because your life may depend on it:** I don't think that we need to comment on this one.

10. **Because it just makes sense:** Having your **Concealed Carry Permit** just makes sense. It's a right thing to do, whether you want greater safety, or just want to know what you're rights are.

1

Concealed Carry In The United States

Concealed carry, **CCW** (carrying a concealed weapon), refers to the practice of carrying a **handgun** or other weapon in public in a concealed manner, either on one's person or in one's proximity.

While there is no federal law specifically addressing the issuance of concealed carry permits, 48 states have passed laws allowing citizens to carry certain concealed firearms in public, either without a permit or after obtaining a permit from state or local law enforcement.

The states give different terms for **licenses** or **permits** to carry a concealed firearm, such as:

1. Concealed Handgun License / Concealed Handgun Permit;

2. Concealed Weapon License / Concealed Weapons Permit / Concealed Defensive Weapons Licence,

3. Concealed Carry Permit / Concealed Carry License;

4. License To Carry / License To Carry Firearms;

5. Carry of Concealed Deadly Weapon License;

6. Concealed Pistol License; etc.

Thirteen states use a single permit to regulate the practices of both **concealed** and **open carry** of a handgun.

Some states publish statistics indicating how many residents hold permits to carry concealed weapons, and their demographics. For example, Florida has issued 1,871,589 permits since adopting its law in 1987, and had 767,739 licensed permit holders as of October 31, 2010.

Reported permit holders are predominantly male. Some states have reported the number of permit holders increasing over time.

The number of permit revocations is typically small.

State laws

Current Status of **Right To Carry** laws

Regulations differ widely by state, with most states currently maintaining a **Shall-Issue** policy. As recently as the mid-'90s most states had been **No-Issue** or **May-Issue**, but over the past 30 years states have consistently adopted less restrictive alternatives.

"Permitting" policies

State regulations relating to the issuance of concealed carry permits generally fall into four categories described as **Unrestricted, Shall Issue, May issue** and **No Issue.**

Unrestricted

An Unrestricted jurisdiction is one in which no **permit** is required to carry a concealed handgun. This is sometimes called a **Constitutional carry** state,

Among U.S. states, only Alaska, Vermont, Arizona, and Wyoming (as of July 1, 2011) allow residents to carry a concealed firearm without a permit.

Alaska is both a **Shall-Issue** and an **Unrestricted** state. Alaska does not require a permit for any law-abiding individual to carry a handgun, either openly or concealed, within the state's borders. However, the state continues to issue permits to any of its residents who meet the state's issuance criteria for **reciprocity** reasons; Alaska residents can **carry** with a permit while in other states that recognize the

Alaska concealed carry license.

Vermont is unique in that permits are not issued for purposes of reciprocity. Since Vermont does not issue permits, its residents are unable to legally **carry concealed** in other states that would normally recognize out-of-state permit holders unless they hold some other state's permit. As a way around this situation, such person who wishes to legally carry a concealed firearm in another state can apply for and receive a non-resident permit from a state that issues non-resident permits, with Florida typically being the state of choice because it holds the widest reciprocity compared with other states that issue non-resident permits. Vermont like Arizona also holds no restrictions as to where the permit holder can carry a weapon. Vermont, Arizona and Wyoming fall outside of **The Federal Gun Free School Zones Act of 1995** which severely limits where an unlicensed person may carry. The license holder may also carry weapons into churches, police stations, and banks with no repercussion.

Arizona is an unrestricted carry state. On April 16, 2010, Arizona Governor **Jan Brewer** signed legislation allowing for unrestricted carry. The law took effect 90 days after the end of the state's current legislative session, putting the effective date on July 29, 2010. Arizona followed the lead of Alaska by continuing to issue permits on a "shall-issue" basis for use by Arizona residents visiting other states.

Effective July 1, 2011, **Wyoming** no longer requires permits for concealed carry by Wyoming residents (in addition to unrestricted open carry, which is currently in effect). Non-Wyoming residents must still obtain a concealed carry permit. The state of Wyoming will continue to issue permits to residents for reciprocity reasons, much as Alaska does.

In **Montana**, **Utah**, **South Carolina**, and **New Hampshire**, bills are being discussed that would allow Vermont style carry.

The Federal Gun Free School Zones Act of 1995 severely limits where an unlicensed person may carry.

Shall-Issue

A Shall-Issue jurisdiction is one that requires a **permit** to carry a concealed handgun, but where the granting of such permits is subject only to *meeting certain criteria laid out in the law*; the granting authority has no discretion in the awarding of the permits. Such laws typically state that a granting authority *shall issue* a permit if the criteria are met, as opposed to laws in which the authority may issue a permit at their discretion.

Typical permit requirements include residency, minimum age, submitting fingerprints, passing a computerized instant background check, attending a certified handgun/firearm safety class, and paying a required fee. These requirements vary widely by jurisdiction.

The following are undisputed Shall-Issue states: **Alaska, Arizona, Arkansas, Colorado, Florida, Georgia, Idaho, Indiana, Iowa, Kansas, Kentucky, Louisiana, Maine, Michigan, Minnesota, Mississippi, Missouri, Montana, Nebraska, Nevada, New Hampshire, New Mexico, North Carolina, North Dakota, Ohio, Oklahoma, Oregon, Pennsylvania, South Carolina, South Dakota, Tennessee, Texas, Utah, Virginia, Washington, West Virginia, and Wyoming.**

The status of **Alabama** and **Connecticut** are in some dispute among gun rights activists. The laws of both states, strictly speaking, would place them in the May-Issue category, as permit issue is by statute discretionary. However, gun rights activists claim that these states are effectively "Shall-Issue" in practice as counties frequently issue permits to applicants who meet certain basic criteria.

Connecticut has a two-tiered permitting system, a local carry permit which is issued on a May-Issue basis, and a state carry permit which is issued on a Shall-Issue basis. Applying for a state weapons carry permit in Connecticut can take up to six months. Firearms owners must first apply for a local carry permit through the local police department, whose willingness to issue such permits may range from No-Issue to Shall-Issue depending on the town (permits are generally easier to obtain in rural areas than in urban areas). The local police department has up to eight weeks to process the local permit application from the time it was submitted to the time the application is adjudicated. If the permit application is denied by the local police department, the applicant may appeal the denial to the Board of Firearms Permit Examiners (BFPE), which must issue a weapons carry permit within 90 days of submission if the applicant meets none of the statutory criteria that would disqualify him or her from holding such permit. Regardless of whether the local permit is granted or denied, the applicant must then apply for a state carry permit, which the BFPE must issue provided the applicant is not disqualified from holding a carry permit by law.

May-Issue

A May-Issue jurisdiction is one that requires a **permit** to carry a concealed handgun, and where the granting of such permits is partially at the discretion of local authorities (frequently the sheriff's department or police). The law typically states that a granting authority *may issue* a permit if various criteria are met. While an applicant must qualify for a permit by meeting criteria defined in state law, local jurisdictions in May-Issue states often have locally-defined requirements that an applicant must meet before a permit will be granted, such as providing adequate justification to the approval authority for needing a concealed carry permit (self-defense in and of itself may not be sufficient justification in some areas where justification is required). A state that is de jure a May-Issue jurisdiction may range anywhere from *No-Issue* to *Shall-Issue* in actual practice.

Alabama, by law, is a *May-Issue* state, but Alabama county sheriffs issue permits to almost all qualified applicants, making it *Shall-Issue* in practice.

California gives wide latitude to the county authorities in issuing permits. In California, the usual issuance of the permits ranges from a *No-Issue* policy, such as **San Francisco**, to an almost Shall-Issue environment in rural areas. However, a permit to carry is generally valid statewide, although local ordinances may prohibit open or concealed carry with or without a permit in some jurisdictions, usually by circumventing state uniform firearms laws by restricting the possession, purchasing, and transporting of ammunition in such jurisdictions.

A gun-owner may apply for a concealed carry permit in a county outside of his or her residence if the applicant's place of business is located there. However to prevent residents of areas with restrictive issuing policies from obtaining permits from jurisdictions with more permissive rules, a business carry permit is only valid in the county where the permit was issued, and the jurisdiction issuing the permit must notify the applicant's home jurisdiction that he or she has a business carry permit in the jurisdiction where his or her workplace is located. For example, a resident of **Yolo County** (which is effectively a "No-Issue" jurisdiction) with a place of business in **Yuba County** (which is a "Shall-Issue" jurisdiction in practice), can obtain a business carry permit in Yuba County. The permit is valid only in Yuba County, and the issuing authority in Yuba County must notify Yolo County that the person has been issued a business weapons carry permit in that county.

Delaware by law is a "May-Issue" state. To obtain a concealed carry permit there is a lengthy application process requiring background checks and sworn, signed statements from 5 references. However, once these steps are completed permits are usually granted. Also, despite the fact that Delaware is a "May-Issue" state there are reciprocity agreements between various states and Delaware which allows many out-of-state residents to legally carry a concealed weapon in Delaware.

In **Hawaii**, carry is allowed with a permit, but it's restricted to "On Duty, In Uniform" and one's employer must register through a local police department. Generally, active and retired peace officers, uniformed security personnel, armored couriers, and Active Duty military members are granted permits.

Maryland law contains provisions for citizens to apply for a concealed carry permit under a limited set of circumstances. These include several occupational reasons such as business owners or their employee who makes large cash deposits, retired police officers, doctors, pharmacists, private detectives, security guards, and railroad police. Correctional officers (who do not require a permit while on duty but cannot carry off duty) may obtain a permit if they can provide legally documented evidence of threats on their life. Similarly, private citizens can obtain a permit if they provide evidence of recent death threats that have been documented by the police. Detractors have complained that the permitting process is capricious, and only those with political or police connections can obtain a permit. However, in recent years the number of permits granted has increased sharply from 4,405 in 2002 to 47,471 in 2010 even though the requirements for obtaining a permit have remained quite strict.

Massachusetts is a May-Issue state for License to Carry Firearms (LTC) "Class A" and "Class B" with the Class A covering 'high capacity' handguns and long arms and the Class B covering 'non-high capacity' handguns and long arms. An LTC grants the holder permission to carry concealed however it can be 'restricted' by the local police chief to curtail that ability. Alternatively, a Firearms Identification Card (FID) is available and covers only non-large capacity rifles or shotguns, ammunition therefor and chemical sprays. A restricted FID for chemical sprays is also available. An FID card does not grant the recipient the ability to carry concealed. Both versions of the FID license are "shall issue".

New Jersey is a May-Issue state, and issues permits to residents and non-residents. Out of a population of 8,000,000 people there are less than 1,000 handgun carry permits in the state (including armed professionals other than law enforcement officers).

New York also gives wide latitude to the county authorities in issuing pistol licenses. In **New York City**, a concealed pistol license is allowed by law, but detractors have claimed it takes a large degree of wealth, political influence, and/or celebrity status to obtain. In contrast, many rural Upstate New

York counties are effectively Shall-Issue in their licensing policies, and some rural upstate counties have policies that allow Unrestricted concealed carry after one has obtained a state carry permit.

Rhode Island law allows for local police chiefs to issue concealed carry permits on a Shall-issue basis, or defer one's permit application to the state Attorney General's Office, which issues permits on a May-issue basis. Currently, nearly all concealed carry applications are sent to the Attorney General's Office for adjudication, thereby placing Rhode Island into the May-Issue category.

No-Issue

A No-Issue jurisdiction is one that **does not** allow any private citizen to carry a concealed handgun. The term refers to the fact that no concealed carry permits will be issued (or recognized).

Illinois, **Wisconsin**, and the **District of Columbia** are No-Issue jurisdictions (although Wisconsin allows **open carry** without a permit whereas Illinois and the District of Columbia **forbid both** open and concealed carry). While technically May-Issue under state law, **Hawaii** and **New Jersey** and certain cities and counties within California and New York are also No-Issue jurisdictions in practice.

Two recent cases in **Wisconsin** have created uncertainty over the enforceability of that state's concealed carry ban. In October 2010 a Clark County judge ruled Wisconsin's concealed carry ban unconstitutional; a Milwaukee County judge also determined the ban to be unconstitutional in February 2011. While concealed carry has the support of the Republican-controlled legislature and Governor **Scott Walker**, a bill permitting concealed carry has yet to be introduced for consideration.

Training requirements

Some states require concealed carry applicants to certify their proficiency with a firearm through some type of training or instruction. Certain training courses developed by the **National Rifle Association** that combine classroom and live-fire instruction typically meet most state training requirements. Some states recognize prior military or police service as meeting training requirements.

Classroom instruction would typically include **firearm** mechanics and terminology, cleaning and maintenance of a firearm, concealed carry legislation and limitations, liability issues, carry methods and safety, home defense, methods for managing and defusing confrontational situations, and practice of gun handling techniques without firing the weapon. Most required CCW training courses devote a considerable amount of time to liability issues.

Depending on the state, a practical component during which the attendee shoots the weapon for the purpose of demonstrating safety and proficiency, may be required. During range instruction, applicants would typically learn and demonstrate safe handling and operation of a firearm and accurate shooting from common self-defense distances. Some states require a certain proficiency to receive a passing grade, whereas other states (e.g., Florida) technically require only a single-shot be fired to demonstrate handgun handling proficiency.

The state of Texas has two levels of its **Concealed Handgun License**: Non-Semi-Auto and Semi-Auto. The permit that is issued depends on the firearm used by the applicant during their practical qualification. An NSA-class CHL restricts the user to revolvers, though single-shot weapons and other curios generally fall into this category. An SA-class CHL allows the holder to carry anything they can conceal, including the class of semi-automatic weapons (having spring-fed magazines and either recoil, blowback or gas-powered operation). NSA-class permits are also severely restricted in reciprocity.

CCW training courses are typically completed in a single day and are good for a set period, the exact duration varying by state. Some states require re-training, sometimes in a shorter, simpler format, for each renewal.

Few states, e.g., South Carolina, recognize the safety and use-of-force training given to military personnel as acceptable in lieu of formal civilian training certification. Such states will ask for a **military ID** (South Carolina) for active persons or **DD214** for legally discharged persons. These few states will commonly request a copy of the applicant's **BTR** (Basic Training Record) proving an up-to-date pistol qualification. Active and retired law enforcement officers are also generally exempt from qualification requirements, due to a federal statute permitting retired law enforcement officers to carry concealed weapons in the United States.

Virginia recognizes eight specific training options to prove competency in handgun handling, ranging from **DD214** for retired military, to certification from law enforcement training, to firearms training conducted by a state or **NRA** certified firearms instructor including electronic, video, or on-line courses. While any one of the eight listed options will be considered adequate proof, individual circuit courts may recognize other training options.

Not all states require training, or hands-on training. For example, **Georgia, Pennsylvania, and Washington** have no training/safety certification requirement.

Reciprocity

Many jurisdictions have established arrangements where they recognize or honor permits or licenses issued by other jurisdictions with comparable standards, for instance in regard to marriage or driver's licenses. This is known as Reciprocity and is based on U.S. Constitution "full faith and credit" provision. Due to the nature of **gun politics**, reciprocity in regard to weapons carry permits or licenses has been controversial.

Reciprocal recognition of concealed carry privileges and rights vary state-to-state, are negotiated between individual states, and sometimes additionally depend on the residency status of the license holder. While 37 states have reciprocity agreements with at least one other state and several states honor all out-of-state concealed carry permits, some states have special requirements like training courses or safety exams, and therefore do not honor permits from states that do not have such requirements for issue. Some states make exceptions for persons under the minimum age (usually 21) if they are active or honorably-discharged members of the military or a police force (the second of these two is also allowed under Federal law). States that do not have this exemption generally do not recognize any license from states that do. An example of this is the State of Washington's refusal to honor any Texas **CHL** as Texas has the military exception to age.

Florida (Resident), Michigan and Missouri hold the widest reciprocity of all the states in the U.S. with the number of other states honoring their permits at 37, followed by Florida (Non-Resident) and Utah at 33; Both Michigan and Missouri, however, do not issue permits to non-residents, and some states that honor Utah permits do *not* extend that to also include Utah's non-resident permits.

Although carry may be legal under State law in accordance with reciprocity agreements, the **Federal Gun Free School Zones Act of 1995** subjects an out-of-state permit holder to federal felony prosecution if they carry a firearm within 1000 feet of any K-12 school's property line. As a result, *it is effectively impossible for a permit holder to legally carry in any developed area outside of the State which physically issued their permit.*

"Opt-Out" statutes ("gun-free zones")

Many states (e.g., Arkansas, Connecticut, Minnesota, Ohio, South Carolina, Georgia, Texas,) allow private businesses to post a specific sign (language and format vary by state) prohibiting concealed carry, violation of which is grounds for revocation of the offender's concealed carry permit. By posting the signs, businesses create areas where it is illegal to carry a concealed handgun similar to regulations concerning schools, hospitals, and public gatherings. In addition to signage, virtually all jurisdictions also allow some form of oral communication by the lawful owner or controller of the property that a person is not welcome and should leave. This notice can be given to anyone for any reason (except for statuses that are protected by Federal **Civil Rights Act of 1964's** such as race), including due to the carrying of firearms by that person, and refusal to heed such a request to leave constitutes trespassing. In some jurisdictions trespass by a person carrying a firearm may have more severe penalties than "simple" trespass.

There is considerable dispute over the effectiveness of

such **"gun-free zones"**. Opponents of such measures, such as **OpenCarry.org**, state that, much like other *malum prohibitum* laws banning gun-related practices, only law-abiding individuals will heed the signage and disarm. Individuals or groups intent on committing far more egregious crimes, such as armed robbery or murder, will not be deterred by signage prohibiting weapons. Further, the reasoning follows that those wishing to commit mass murder might *intentionally* choose gun-free venues like shopping malls, schools and churches (where weapons carry is generally prohibited) because the population inside is disarmed and thus less able to stop them.

In some states, business owners have been documented posting signs that appear to prohibit guns, but legally do not because the signs do not meet state or local laws defining the appearance, placement, or verbiage of the sign. Such signage can be posted out of ignorance to the law, or intent to pacify gun control advocates while not actually prohibiting the practice.

Federal law
Gun Control Act of 1968

The Gun Control Act passed by Congress in 1968 lists felons, illegal aliens, and other codified persons as prohibited from purchasing or possessing firearms. During the application process for concealed carry states carry out thorough background checks to prevent these individuals from obtaining permits. Additionally the Brady Handgun Violence Prevention Act created an FBI maintained system in 1994 for instantly checking the backgrounds of potential firearms buyers in an effort to prevent these individuals from obtaining weapons.

Law Enforcement Officer's Safety Act

In 2004, the United States Congress enacted the Law Enforcement Officers Safety Act (LEOSA), 18 U.S. Code 926B and 926C. This federal law allows two classes of persons—the "qualified law enforcement officer" and the "qualified retired law enforcement officer"—to carry a concealed firearm in any jurisdiction in the United States, regardless of any state or local law to the contrary, with certain exceptions.

Gun Free School Zones Act of 1995

The Federal Gun Free School Zone Act of 1995 severely limits where a person may legally carry a firearm. It does this by making it generally unlawful for an armed citizen to be within 1000 feet (extending out from the property lines) of a place that the individual knows, or has reasonable cause to believe, is a K-12 school. Although a State-issued carry permit may exempt a person from this restriction in the State that physically issued their permit, it does not exempt them in other States which recognize their permit under reciprocity agreements made with the issuing State. The law's failure to provide adequate protection to LEOSA qualified officers, licensed concealed carry permit holders, and other armed citizens, is an issue that the United States Congress so far has not addressed.

Federal Property

Some Federal statutes restrict the carrying of firearms on the premises of certain Federal properties such as military installations or land controlled by the USACE (United States Army Corps of Engineers).

National Park Carry

On May 22, 2009, President Barrack Obama signed H.R. 627, the "Credit Card Accountability Responsibility and Disclosure Act of 2009," into law. The bill contained an amendment introduced by Senator Tom Coburn (R-OK) that prohibits the Secretary of the Interior from enacting or enforcing any regulations that restrict possession of firearms in National Parks or Wildlife Refuges, as long as the person complies with laws of the state in which the unit is found. This provision was supported by the National Rifle Association and opposed by the Brady Campaign to Prevent Gun Violence, the National Parks Conservation Association, and the Coalition of National Park Service Retirees, among other organizations. As of February 2010 concealed handguns are for the first time legal in all but 3 of the nation's 391 national parks and wildlife refuges so long as all applicable federal, state, and local regulations are adhered to. Previously firearms were allowed into parks non-concealed and unloaded.

Full Faith and Credit (CCW Permits)

Attempts were made in the 110th Congress, United States House of Representatives (H.R.226) and the United States Senate (S.388), to enact legislation to compel complete reciprocity for concealed carry licenses. Opponents of national reciprocity have pointed out that this legislation would effectively require states with higher standards of permit issuance (i.e., training courses, safety exams, good cause, etc.) to honor permits from states with more liberal issuance policies.

Legal issues
Court rulings

Prior to the 1897 supreme court case *Robertson v. Baldwin,* the federal courts had been silent on the issue of concealed carry. In the dicta from a maritime law case the Supreme Court commented that state laws restricting concealed weapons do not infringe upon the right to bear arms protected by the Federal Second Amendment.

In the majority decision in the 2008 Supreme Court case of *District of Columbia v. Heller*, Justice Antonin Scalia wrote;

"Like most rights, the Second Amendment right is not unlimited. It is not a right to keep and carry any weapon whatsoever in any manner whatsoever and for whatever purpose: For example, concealed weapons prohibitions have been upheld under the Amendment or state analogues ... The majority of the 19th-century courts to consider the question held that prohibitions on carrying concealed weapons were lawful under the Second Amendment or state analogues."

Heller was a landmark case because for the first time in United States history a Supreme Court decision defined the right to bear arms as constitutionally guaranteed to private citizens rather than a right restricted to "well regulated militia[s]". The Justices asserted that sensible restrictions on the right to bear arms are constitutional however an outright ban on a specific type of firearm, in this case handguns, was in fact unconstitutional. The decision is limited because it only applies to federal enclaves such as the District of Columbia.

On June 28, 2010, the U.S. Supreme Court struck down the handgun ban enacted by the city of Chicago, Illinois, in *McDonald v. Chicago*, effectively extending the Heller decision to states and local governments nationwide. Banning handguns in any jurisdiction has the effect of rendering invalid any licensed individual's right to carry concealed in that area except for federally exempted retired and current law enforcement officers and other government employees acting in the discharge of their official duties.

Legal liability

Even when self-defense is justified, there can be serious civil or criminal liabilities related to self-defense when a concealed carry permit holder brandishes or fires his/her weapon. For example, if innocent bystanders are hurt or killed, there could be both civil and criminal liabilities even if the use of deadly force was completely justified. Some states also technically allow an assailant who is shot by a gun owner to bring civil action. In some states, liability is present when a resident brandishes the weapon, threatens use, or exacerbates a volatile situation, or when the resident is carrying while intoxicated. **It is important to note that simply pointing a firearm at any person constitutes felony assault with a deadly weapon unless circumstances validate a demonstration of force.** A majority of states who allow concealed carry, however, forbid suits being brought in such cases, either by barring lawsuits for damages resulting from a criminal act on the part of the plaintiff, or by granting the gun owner immunity from such a civil suit if it is found that he or she was justified in shooting.

Simultaneously, increased passage of **Castle Doctrine** laws allow persons who own firearms and/or carry them concealed to use them without first attempting to retreat. **Castle Doctrine** (a.k.a. **Defense of Habitation Law**) is an American legal doctrine arising from English Common Law that designates one's place of residence (or, in some states, any place legally occupied, such as one's car or place of work) as a place in which one enjoys protection from illegal trespassing and violent attack. It gives a person the legal right to use deadly force to defend that place (his "castle") and any other innocent persons legally inside it, from violent attack or an intrusion which may lead to violent attack.

In a legal context, therefore, use of deadly force which actually results in death may be defended as justifiable homicide under the Castle Doctrine. Castle Doctrines are legislated by the state though not all states in the US have a Castle Doctrine law.

Nevertheless many states have adopted escalation of force laws along with provisions for concealed carry. These include the necessity to first verbally warn a trespasser or lay hands on a trespasser before a shooting is justified (unless the trespasser is armed or assumed to be so). This escalation of force does not apply if the shooter reasonably believes a violent felony has been or is about to be committed on the property by the trespasser. Additionally some states have a duty to retreat provision which requires a permit holder, especially in public places, to vacate him or herself from a potentially dangerous situation before resorting to deadly force. The duty to retreat does not restrictively apply in a person's home or business though escalation of force may be required. In 1895 the Supreme Court ruled in *Beard v. U.S.* that if an individual does not provoke an assault and is residing in a place they have a right to be then they may use considerable force against someone they reasonably believe may do them serious harm without being charged with murder or manslaughter should that person be killed. However in all states except for Texas lethal force is not justifiable solely for the purpose of defending property. In those 49 states, lethal force is only authorized when serious harm is presumed to be imminent.

Even given these relaxed restrictions on use of force, using a handgun must still be a last resort in some jurisdictions; meaning the user must reasonably believe that nothing short of deadly force will protect the life or property at stake in a situation. Additionally, civil liabilities for errors that cause harm to others still exist, although civil immunity is provided in the Castle Doctrine laws of some states (e.g., Texas).

Penalties for carrying illegally

Main article: Weapon possession (crime)

Typical policies that are used to determine who can legally carry concealed weapons are a prohibition of concealed carry, discretionary licensing, non-discretionary licensing, minimum age requirements (e.g., 18 or 21 years), successful completion of an instructor-led course, and marksmanship/handling qualification on a firing range. Less common is unregulated, legal concealed carry such as in Vermont, Alaska, and Arizona.

In the United States no convicted felon may purchase, transfer, or otherwise be in the possession of any firearm. Illegally concealing a handgun is a felony in many states therefore conviction of such a crime would automatically result in the forfeiture of a citizen's gun rights for life nationwide. Additional state penalties for unlawful carry of a concealed firearm can be severe with punishments including expensive fines, extended jail time, loss of voting rights, and even passport cancellation. A federal penalty of ten years in prison has been enacted for those found to be in possession of either firearms or ammunition while subject to a protection or restraining order. Such an order is grounds for the revocation of any concealed carry permit and the outright denial of any person's new application while the order is active. Weapon possession, in the context of concealed weapons, is a crime of that circumstance in which a person who is not legally authorized to carry a concealed weapon is found in possession of such a weapon. In the United States this can also be interpreted as the possession of a firearm by a person legally disqualified from doing so under the Gun Control Act. These prohibited individuals include those who have been dishonorably discharged from the military, those who have been convicted of misdemeanor domestic violence, unlawful immigrant aliens, and individuals who have renounced their United States citizenship. None of these individuals are eligible for concealed weapons permits and may be punished not only for unlawful concealed carry of a handgun but also for unlawful possession of a firearm. Depending on state law, it can also apply to concealed carry of otherwise illegal knives such as stilettos, dirks or switchblades.

Citizens holding concealed carry permits may be prosecuted for failing to adhere to state and federal rules and regulations concerning the lawful exercise of carrying a concealed weapon. Some states do not allow the carrying of more than one concealed firearm by permit holders. Concealing two handguns, for example, might constitute a violation of law resulting in permit revocation or criminal charges. Carrying a handgun in the glove box of a vehicle, though commonly regarded as safe and legal, is considered illegal concealment in some states and could be punishable as a felony offense among non-permit holders. When arrested for any firearms offense the weapon(s) in question will be confiscated and could be destroyed upon conviction. While legally carrying concealed outside of one's particular state of residence, such as in a state which grants reciprocity to the bearer's permit, he or she must comply with all regulations in the state in which they are currently carrying even if those rules and regulations differ from those of the individual's permit issuing state. Some states require that a person carrying a concealed weapon immediately declare this fact to any law enforcement officer they may encounter in the line of their official duties. This provision most commonly applies to traffic stops and police questioning but is also required upon approach of an officer by the person who is carrying concealed. Failure to comply with this provision is an arrestable misdemeanor and additionally may require the mandatory revocation of the licensee's permit. However simply passing an officer on the street, even at close distance, does not generally require the declaration of a concealed weapon. Carry of a concealed weapon by a licensed individual where prohibited is also generally referred to as illegal weapon possession. In some states, no person may be in the public possession of a firearm while under the intoxicating effects of narcotics (whether prescribed or otherwise) or alcohol (usually defined as .01% BAC but up to .05% BAC in some areas).

Even in localities where concealed carrying is permitted, there may be legal restrictions on where a person may carry a concealed weapon unless state law overrides a business posting that no firearms are allowed.

Examples include the prohibition of concealed carry in some states at:

• Public or private elementary and secondary schools either inside or within 1,000 feet of these areas (the Federal Gun-Free School Zones Act of 1990 contains an exception for individuals carrying under a state-issued permit, but some states that issue permits forbid carry in school buildings and/or on school property. The law authorizes federal penalties of up to $5,000 and five years in prison upon conviction.)

• Establishments that sell alcohol. The interpretation of this restriction varies widely from state to state. Some ban carry from all such establishments such as retail liquor stores and supermarkets, others only from businesses that sell alcohol "by the drink" for on-premises consumption such as restaurants (with some of these states, such as Kentucky, further distinguishing by banning carry in bar areas but not in dining areas), still others only from businesses falling under the state's definition of a "bar" or "nightclub".

• Government buildings (State Capitol, courthouses, police stations, federal buildings, post offices).

• Public accommodations (theaters, concert halls, indoor shopping malls).

• Public events (polling places, state fairs, stadiums and other sporting venues).

The city of Chicago, Illinois as well as the District of Columbia had banned handguns completely within their respective jurisdictions. However, two recent Supreme Court cases have effectively deemed those statutes to be illegal (see above).

Lastly, some states regulate which firearms may be concealed by a particular permit holder. Texas, for example, differentiates between semi-automatic and non-semi-automatic firearms, and an "NSA"-class permit holder cannot carry an autoloading handgun (restricting them largely to revolvers). Texans who qualify with a revolver are only allowed to carry a revolver; if they qualify with a semi-automatic, they can carry either a semi-automatic or a revolver. Other restrictions seen in certain states include restricting the user to a gun no more powerful than they used when qualifying, or to one or more specific guns specified by the permit holder when applying. New York prohibits certain specific makes and models of pistols (mostly Saturday Night Specials) and will not issue a permit for those specific weapons. Maryland has banned Saturday Night Specials completely. Other states ban the carrying of handguns with large-capacity magazines. In most states, though, a CCW permit holder is limited only by what they can conceal while wearing particular clothing.

2
Research on the Effects
of Concealed Carry

In Florida, which in 1987 introduced the "shall-issue" concealed carry law used as a model for other states, one study found that crimes committed against residents dropped markedly upon the general issuance of concealed-carry licenses. However, another study suggests that in most states with shall-issue laws, there were increases in crime of all types.

In a 1998 book, *More Guns, Less Crime*, economics researcher John Lott's analysis of crime report data claims a statistically significant effect of concealed carry laws on crime, with more permissive concealed carry laws correlated with a decrease in overall crime. Lott studied crime statistics from 1977 to 1993 and found that the passage of concealed carry laws resulted in a murder rate reduction of 8.5%, rape rate reduction of 5%, and aggravated assault reduction of 7%.

In a 2003 article, Yale Law professors John J. Donohue III and Ian Ayres have claimed that Lott's conclusions were largely the result of a limited data set and that re-running Lott's tests with more complete data (and nesting the separate Lott and Mustard level and trend econometric models to create a hybrid model simultaneously calculating level and trend) yielded none of the results Lott claimed. However Lott has recently updated his findings with further evidence. According to the FBI, during the first year of the Obama administration the national murder rate declined by 7.4% along with other categories of crime which fell by significant percentages. During that same time national gun sales increased dramatically. According to Mr. Lott 450,000 more people bought guns in November 2008 than November 2007 which represents a 40% increase in sales, a trend which continued throughout 2009. The drop in the murder rate was the biggest one-year drop since 1999, another year when gun sales soared in the wake of increased calls for gun control as a result of the Columbine shooting.

In reporting on Lott's original analysis *The Chronicle of Higher Education* has said that although his findings are controversial "Mr. Lott's research has convinced his peers of at least one point: No scholars now claim that legalizing concealed weapons causes a major increase in crime."

The National Research Council, the working arm of the National Academy of Sciences, claims to have found "no credible evidence" either supporting or disproving Lott's thesis. However, James Q. Wilson wrote a dissenting opinion in which he argued that all of the Committee's own estimates confirmed Lott's finding that right-to-carry laws had decreased the murder rate and most of Lott's statistical analysis was inscrutable and survive virtually every reanalysis done by the committee. On the Ayres and Donohue hybrid model showing more guns-more crime, the NAS panel stated: "The committee takes no position on whether the hybrid model provides a correct description of crime levels or the effects of right-to-carry laws."

A 2008 article by Carlisle E. Moody and Thomas B. Marvell uses a more extensive data set and projects effects of the Ayres and Donohue hybrid model beyond a five-year span. Though their data set renders an apparent reduction in the cost of crime, Donohue and Ayres point out that the cost of crime increased in 23 of the 24 jurisdictions under scrutiny. Florida was the only jurisdiction showing positive effects from Shall-Issue Laws. Donohue and Ayres question the special case of Florida as well.

Using publicly available media reports, the Violence Policy Center claims that from May 2007 through the end of 2009, concealed carry permit holders in the U.S. have killed at least 117 individuals, including 9 law enforcement officers (excluding cases where individuals were acquitted, but including pending cases). There were about 25,000 murders by firearm that period, meaning that concealed carry permit holders committed less than 1% of the murders by firearm. Furthermore, a large number of the victims were killed in extended suicides, most of which took place in the home of the shooter, where arms can be possessed without special permits.

According to FBI police crime reports, in 2008 there were 16,272 murders and 245 legally justified/self defense killings in the United States. However, the FBI Uniform Crime Report states that the justifiable homicide statistic does not represent eventual adjudication by medical examiner, coroner, district attorney, grand jury, trial jury or appellate court; few US jurisdictions allow a police crime report to adjudicate a homicide as justifiable, resulting in a undercount in the UCR table. The vast majority of defensive gun uses (DGUs) do not involve killing or even wounding an attacker, with government surveys showing 108,000 (NCVS) to 23 million (raw NSPOF) DGUs per year, with ten private national surveys showing 764,000 to 3.6 million DGU per year.

In 2009, Public Health Law Research, an independent organization, published an evidence summary concluding there is not enough evidence to establish the effectiveness of "Shall-Issue" laws as a public health intervention to reduce violent crime.

This empirical back-and-forth may well indicate that the data is too incomplete, ambiguous, and crude to establish the positive or negative effects of conceal-carry on crime. For further discussion, also see Moody and Marvel's and Ayres and Donohue's 2009 articles in Econ Journal Watch.

3
Open Carry In The United States

Open carry in the United States is shorthand terminology for **openly carrying a firearm in public,** as contrasted with **concealed carry,** where firearms cannot be seen by the casual observer.

The practice of open carry, where gun owners **openly** carry firearms while they go about their daily business, has seen an increase in the U.S. in recent years.

In the last decade, this has been marked by a number of organized events intended to increase the visibility of open carry and public awareness about the practice. Critics of open carry, on the other hand, have raised concerns about right-wing extremism and the threat of armed revolt against the government of the United States.

Encouraged by groups like OpenCarry.org and GeorgiaCarry.org — and some participants of the Free State Project — open carry has seen a revival in recent years. As of 2010, it is not yet clear if this represents a sea change, or just a short-term trend. Open carry is strongly opposed by gun control groups such as the Brady Campaign and the Coalition to Stop Gun Violence.

Proponents of open carry point to history and statistics, noting that criminals usually conceal their weapons: The 2006 FBI study "Violent Encounters: A Study of Felonious Assaults on Our Nation's Law Enforcement Officers" by Anthony Pinizzotto revealed that criminals carefully conceal their firearms and they eschew the use of holsters.

The open carry movement has had mixed reception in the gun rights community. Alan Gottlieb of the Second Amendment Foundation and the NRA have been cautious in expressing support for open carry, while special-interest groups such as the aforementioned OpenCarry.org and GeorgiaCarry.org, state-level groups such as the Texas State Rifle Association (TSRA), and certain national groups such as the Gun Owners of America (GOA) have been more outspoken in favor of the practice.

Jurisdictions in the United States
In the United States, the laws concerning open carry vary by state and sometimes by municipality.

Open carry laws of loaded handguns
Gold Star Open Carry State laws
Open Carry Friendly State laws
Licensed Open Carry State laws
Non Permissive Open Carry State laws
Rural Open Carry State laws

Definitions
Open carry
The act of publicly carrying a firearm in *plain sight.*
Plain sight
Broadly defined as *not being hidden from common view;* varies somewhat from state to state.
Preemption
In the context of open carry: the act of a state legislature passing laws which eliminate or limit or the ability of local municipalities to regulate the possession or carrying of firearms.

Prohibited persons

People prohibited by law from carrying a firearm. Typical examples are felons, those convicted of a misdemeanor or domestic violence, those found to be addicted to alcohol or drugs, and those who have been involuntarily committed to a mental institution.

Categories of law

Today in the United States, the laws vary from state to state regarding open carry of firearms. The categories are defined as follows:

Permissive open carry states

A state that has passed full preemption of all firearms laws. They permit open carry to all non-prohibited citizens without permit or license. Also open carry is lawful on foot and in a motor vehicle. The term carries a pro-gun bias, as gun-control advocacy groups like the Brady Center generally give such states very low "scores" on their own ratings systems.

Licensed open carry states

A state that has passed full preemption of all firearms laws. They also permit open carry of a handgun to all non-prohibited citizens once they have been issued a permit or license. Also open carry of a handgun is lawful on foot and in a motor vehicle.

Anomalous open carry states

In these states, open carry of a handgun is generally lawful, but the state may lack preemption or there may be other significant restrictions. The limitations and/or lack of pre-emption means that certain of these states are, in their judicial system and law enforcement societies, not very "friendly" towards the practice.

Non-permissive open carry states

In these states, open carry of a handgun is not lawful, or is only lawful under such a limited set of circumstances that public carry is otherwise prohibited. Such limited circumstances may include open carry when hunting or while traveling to/from hunting locations, and while on property controlled by the person carrying, or for lawful self-defense.

Six states and the District of Columbia fully prohibit the open carry of handguns. On the other side, twelve states permit open carry of a handgun without requiring the citizen to apply for any permit or license. Thirteen states require some form of permit (often the same permit as allows a person to carry concealed), and the remaining seventeen states, though not prohibiting the practice in general, do not preempt local laws or law enforcement policies, and/or have significant restrictions on the practice, such as prohibiting it within the boundaries of an incorporated urban area. California requires openly carried firearms to be unloaded if being possessed in a county with more than 250,000 residents. Illinois allows Open carry in unincorporated areas and on private property only.

As of August, 2009, four states that currently restrict open carry as a remnant of the post-Civil war Reconstruction era (Texas, South Carolina, Oklahoma and Arkansas) are considering making it again legal. A bill was drafted in the Texas Legislature for the 2009 session, but did not make it out of committee; proponents such as OpenCarry.org and the Texas State Rifle Association hope to reintroduce similar legislation in the 2011 session.

Constitutional implications

Open carry has never been ruled out as a right under the Second Amendment of the U.S. Constitution by any court. In the majority opinion in the case of *District of Columbia v. Heller* (2008), Justice Antonin Scalia wrote concerning the entirety of the elements of the Second Amendment, ***"We find that the elements of the Second Amendment guarantee the individual right to possess and carry weapons in case of confrontation."***

However, Scalia continued, ***"Like most rights, the Second Amendment right is not unlimited. It is not a right to keep and carry any weapon whatsoever in any manner whatsoever and for whatever purpose."***

Forty-three states' constitutions recognize and secure the right to keep and bear arms in some form, and none of those prohibit the open carrying of firearms. Five state constitutions provide that the state legislature may regulate the manner of carrying or bearing arms, and advocates argue that none rule out open carry specifically. Nine states' constitutions indicate that the *concealed* carrying of firearms may be regulated and/or prohibited by the state legislature. Open carry advocates argue that, by exclusion, open carrying of arms may *not* be legislatively controlled in these states. But this is not settled law.

Section 1.7 of Kentucky's state constitution only empowers the state to enact laws prohibiting "concealed carry".

4
The Five Stages Of Violent Crime

By Anonymous.

I am a firm believer in this defense theology and urge anyone who carries a firearm for protection (and even those who do not) to read this report carefully. A violent crime does not begin when one person with ill intent draws a weapon or attacks another.

Stages of Violent Crime:
1. Intent
2. Interview
3. Positioning
4. Attack
5. Reaction

I do not believe the act begins after the attacker has made his intentions known by drawing his weapon on you; it began when he formed his intent.

Well, there's not a lot one can do personally to stop another's intent, so we need to look further in the sequence and try to derail the train before it gets to the attack.

For the sake of argument, let's remove weapons from the equation for just a moment.

A 5'2" tall attacker isn't going to choose a 6'6" tall victim over a 5'1" tall victim. He's going to attack the easier target.

Now let's add back the weapons. Concealed carry presumes that it is better to wait until the opponent has drawn his knife or gun and then try to 'fix' the situation. It seems a bit risky to think that it's better to attempt to stop a violent crime in the fourth stage when you could prevent it in the second.

A concealed weapon cannot deter an attack at the 'interview' stage; it's completely ineffectual in that role. Open carry is the only method that provides a direct deterrent.

Let's say the bad-guy missed the openly carried pistol and holster during the interview stage, and has proceeded to the 'positioning' stage. Chances are pretty good he'll see it at some point then, right? Then, for whatever reason, he begins his attack despite your openly carried sidearm.

At this point, the open carrier is on level footing with the concealed carrier, the attack has begun. Who has the advantage? Well, with all things being equal (skill level and equipment) the open carrier has a speed of draw advantage over the concealed carrier.

First One To Be Shot:

There are some who criticize open carry and claim it will make you more of a target or "the first one shot" when a robber walks into the 7-11, despite the absolute lack of evidence that this has ever happened. If the robber walks in and sees that you're armed, his whole plan has encountered an unexpected variable.

In bank robberies where he might expect to see an armed guard he will have already factored that possibility into his plan, but only for the armed guard, not for open or concealed carry citizens. No robber robs a bank without at least a rudimentary plan.

Nevertheless, being present for a bank robbery is an extremely remote possibility for most of us regardless of our preferred method of handgun carry, so let's go back to the 7-11. If the robber sees that someone is armed he is forced to either significantly alter his plan or abort it outright.

Robbery is an inherently apprehensive occupation; one that doesn't respond well to instant modifications. An assailant is not prepared to commit murder when he only planned for larceny. He knows that petty larceny will not garner the intense police manhunt that a murder would.

He doesn't know if you're an armed citizen, or a police officer, and isn't going to take the time to figure it out. Either way, if someone in the 7-11 is unexpectedly armed, how many others might be similarly adorned, and where might they be? Does this unexpectedly armed individual have a partner who is likewise armed nearby, someone who is watching him right now? Self preservation compels him to abort the plan for one that is less risky.

So we see that the logic matches the history; open carriers are not the first ones shot because it doesn't make sense in any common street crime scenario that they would be. If your personal self protection plan emphasizes "Hollywood" style crimes over the more realistic street mugging, it might be best to stay home.

Surprise:

Probably the most common condemnation of open carry comes from the armchair tacticians who believe it's better to have the element of surprise in a criminal encounter. Although this was touched on in the previous paragraph about deterrence, I'll expand on it specifically here because there are some important truths you need to consider before you lean too heavily on this false support.

Surprise as a defensive tactic is often based on unrealistic or ill-thought out scenarios, and seems to exist only in the minds of concealed carry firearms proponents. The circumstance where several street toughs surround and taunt you for a while before robbing you, like in some Charles Bronson movie, is not realistic; the mugger wants to get in and get out as fast as possible. In most cases you will have only seconds to realize what's happening, make a decision, and react.

Imagine you're walking along the sidewalk when two gangster looking teenagers suddenly appear at the corner coming in the opposite direction. You have only seconds to react if their intent is to victimize you. Do you draw your concealed firearm now? or wait until there's an actual visible threat?

If they are just on their way to church and you pull a gun on them, *you* become the criminal and you will likely forever lose your firearms rights for such a foolish act. If you don't draw and they pull a knife or pistol when they're just a couple of steps away, your only options are to draw (if you think you can) or comply.

Imagine staring at the shiny blade of a knife being held by a nervous and violent mugger, three inches from your or your wife's throat and having to decide whether or not you have time to draw from concealment. The element of surprise may not do you any good; in fact the only surprising thing that might happen is that your concealed carry pistol gets taken from you along with your wallet.

The thug may later get a good chuckle with his buddies about how you brought a gun to a knife fight.

The simple truth is that while surprise is a monumentally superior tactical maneuver, it is exclusively an *offensive* action, not a defensive one.

What many internet commandos call "defensive surprise" is nothing more than damage control, a last ditch effort to fight your way back out of a dangerous situation.

I am not aware of any army that teaches using surprise as a defense against attack. No squad of soldiers goes on patrol with their weapons hidden so that they can "surprise" the enemy should they walk into an ambush.

It Will Get Stolen:

Another common criticism of open carry is that the firearm itself will be the target of theft, prompting a criminal to attack simply to get the gun from you. Like the previous example of being the first one shot in a robbery, this is despite the fact that there is no credible evidence it happens.

It also ignores the more obvious fact that anything you possess can make you the target of a crime, be it a car, a watch, or even a female companion (girlfriend, wife, or daughter). Crooks commonly steal for only one of two reasons; to get something you have that they want, or to get something that you have so that they can sell it and buy something they want.

I don't claim this could never happen; just that it's so remote a possibility that it doesn't warrant drastic alterations to our strategy of self defense. If you believe otherwise, leave your wife, children, watch, sunglasses, jewelry, and cell phone at home, hop into your Pinto wagon, and head out to do your thing alone.

Very often, someone critical of open carry will cite some example of a uniformed police officer whose gun was taken by a violent criminal, and yes, this does indeed happen. The argument, however, breaks down when they assume the officer was targeted solely to steal his gun. What is more likely is that the officer was targeted merely for being a uniformed police officer and the gun was stolen as a by-product of the attack.

More often, the officer's gun is taken during the struggle to get the suspect into custody due to an entirely unrelated matter. However, let's suppose, for argument, that a police officer really was attacked just to get his firearm.

What actions did the police department take to prevent it from reoccurring? Did they demand that their officers carry concealed? No, of course not. You should, like the police, prioritize your defense strategy for the most likely threat first, and the least likely last.

It Scares People:

One other statement against open carry I hear is that it damages public perception of firearms owners; that by carrying openly we are not being good ambassadors to the public.

While there are some people who have a genuine fear of firearms, due either to some horrible past experience or anti-gun indoctrination, the majority of people are either indifferent to them or quite fascinated by them.

I've never kept track of the dozens of fellow citizens I've encountered who have marveled at the idea of open carry, but I do know exactly how many have expressed displeasure at it; only one.

People are scared of many things for many reasons; however, pretending those things do not exist only perpetuates the fear. Someone who is disturbed by open carry is going to be every bit as disturbed by concealed carry. The only effective way to overcome a fear is to come to the intellectual realization that the phobia is based on emotion and not on fact.

By being a firsthand witness that a firearm was carried responsibly and peaceably, and wasn't being carried in the commission of a crime, one who was apprehensive about firearms discovers their fear is not based on fact, but emotion. Thus, open carry can be a very effectual way of helping to overcome emotionally based fear of the firearm. After all, you'd be much more likely to believe in ghosts if you saw one rather than if you only heard a ghost story around a campfire.

In other words, we give significantly more credibility to the things we experience than we do to the things we hear. The bottom line is that this argument is made by people who don't, can't, or haven't carried openly. Those of us who do on a regular basis have an entirely different experience.

I'm Not Comfortable Carrying Openly:

This is really the only reasonable argument against open carry for an individual. We all have a comfort zone for any aspect of our lives and we prefer to stay within that comfort zone. Most all agree that it's better to be armed and never need the firearm than it is to need it and not have it.

There is a point where concealing your firearm becomes so problematic, due to conditions like temperature or comfort, that some choose to either leave it behind or carry in such a way that it would be difficult or impossible to draw it quickly.

If it takes me five or six seconds to draw my firearm from deep concealment and I had sufficient time before hand to actually do so, I would prefer to use that five or six seconds to avoid the entire encounter.

I'm glad we have concealed carry laws in most of the states; it empowers and protects not only us but the general public through the offset deterrent effect. Some of us, however, choose the more direct deterrent effect of open carry.

Conclusion

No, open carry is not the be-all-end-all of self defense any more than is concealed carry. The purpose of this report is not to convince you to carry a firearm openly, but merely to point out the reasoning I used to determine that it is often the best option for me. If you think otherwise, please feel free to write an essay of your own outlining the reasoning you used.

I would suggest that you avoid the intellectual mistake of emphasizing rare or unlikely defense scenarios that many of us will never experience. I believe one should prioritize for the most likely threat, not the least likely threat.

I don't put Hollywood style bank robberies high on my threat list because I rarely go into a bank and those types of robberies are very rare themselves. I live in the most crime riddled city in the northwest. The most likely threat here is some young male with a knife or gun trying to carjack me or mug me on the street, in the park, or in a parking lot.

With this knowledge I build my personal self protection plan based on that manner of attack. This may not suit you, especially if you live in Hollywood, U.S.A.

5
Open Carry Argument

By Anonymous.

My primary goal when I'm out and about, in addition to whatever I go out and about to do, is to go about my business peaceably and not be the victim of a violent crime. To that end I carry a firearm when I go out and follow all the standard safety practices of gun ownership like maintaining situational awareness, staying out of high crime areas, and avoiding confrontation. I also have the larger goal of making it through life without shooting anyone. Simply put, I don't want to be responsible, legally or morally, for another man's death. Those two goals might appear at first to be mutually exclusive, and with concealed carry it would be a difficult set of goals to realize.

Carry of any weapon for defensive purposes is a solemn responsibility. Those of us who do (openly or concealed) are mortified by the idea that our behavior is more reckless because we are armed. That simply because we carry a handgun we take more risks than we would if we were unarmed.

While it would be presumptuous to claim that we are all responsible gun owners, I believe that the vast majority of gun owners are. Regardless of what or how you carry, you need to realize that you are setting yourself up to lose. Whenever you are placed in a defensive situation, you will always lose; it's only the degree of loss that's negotiable.

Massad Ayoob, in his book, *In The Gravest Extreme,* suggests that you toss the robber a wad of cash and move off, even if you could prevail with a weapon. There's a very good reason for this.

Regardless of how skilled you are at drawing your weapon, you are going to lose.

It may be only a *minor* loss, like being very shaken up and not sleeping well for a few days, or it may be a *major* loss, like becoming fertilizer, or (most likely) it may be somewhere in-between, but you always lose. Your life will not be the same even if you prevail.

Carrying a concealed firearm appears to a criminal that you are unarmed. Every study I've ever read, claims that criminals will avoid an armed person, or home, when selecting a victim. That only makes sense, right?

Robbers, rapists, or carjackers might be dumb and opportunistic, but they have the same instinctual sense of self preservation all of us have. Hyenas don't attack lions to steal the gazelle the lions have just killed. It's all about risk management; are the potential gains (a tasty gazelle dinner) worth the risks (of the pain and damage the lion's teeth will cause), and does the hyena really need to test the lion to figure out the answer? No, the hyena can see the lion's teeth and knows to stay well clear.

Deterrent Value:

When I'm carrying concealed, I feel like my 'teeth' are hidden, and thus of no real deterrent value. If I *appear* unarmed, I am unarmed in the eyes of the robber, I look like as easy a target as anyone else out on the street.

My probability of being a victim of a crime, violent or otherwise, is completely unchanged by the fact that I have hidden beneath my shirt the means to my self-defence.

My goal, however, is not to be a victim in the first place, remember? I don't want to be a victim who fought back successfully and triumphed; I prefer to not be victimized at all.

I recognize that there are some people who (think they) want to be victimized so they can whip out their concealed firearm and 'surprise' the mugger. That is, in my opinion, foolish immaturity.

Concealed carry is good; it throws a wrench in the works for criminals who might see the teeming masses as a smorgasbord of financial gain. The deterrent effect, nonetheless, is indirect and often nil. At some point the thug will weigh the risks vs. the gains; is his current need for money/drugs/booze/gold greater than the gamble that one of those people might be carrying a gun? If he decides to play the odds, which with surprise tip the scale in his favor, he will attack. Will his attack allow enough time for me to draw my concealed firearm to affect a defense? Maybe, but then again, maybe not.

Remember, I don't want to be a victim and I don't want to shoot anyone.

So how do I realize both goals; or how do I make them inclusive? I can do that through open carry. By making it obvious that I am armed, that I have teeth, I tip the risk scale so that the criminal's risk far outweighs any possible gains. There is no question when the thug is doing his risk assessment. There's something right there in plain sight that can quickly and painfully change, or terminate his life.

He has the same sense of self preservation as any other living creature and to him his life is every bit as valuable as yours is to you. I think it would be foolish to ignore this fact when you develop your overall strategy.

6
My Personal OC Rules

By Forrest Brown

One of the reasons I "open-carry" daily is to raise the visibility of our movement and encourage discussion.

I know quite well that people are going to have a reaction to my firearm, which is exactly what happened today at the grocery store. The woman working at the register said something I've gotten used to hearing, but she phrased it a little differently than I expected to hear.

"I see a man with a gun, but no badge. What's wrong with this picture?"

I wasn't sure if she was trying to offer misguided legal advice or ask me in a roundabout way if I'm a law enforcement officer. I decided the best option was to start with the facts.

"Nothing that I can see. Open-carry is legal in Maine."

She asked if I had a permit for the gun. The gun? I chose not to mention that I have a CFP (Concealed Firearm Permit); I didn't see it as relevant to the discussion.

"The Maine state Constitution is my gun permit. Article 1, section 16. It's very unambiguous, and grants this right to every citizen."

Another customer had come up behind me in line, so I asked the cashier to have a nice day and, transaction concluded, went about my business.

This is a conversation I seem to have a lot with people. I'm not sure if it's driven by fear of guns or just ignorance of the law, though it's probably a combination of both. What I hope that I've accomplished by the end of the conversation is an adjustment of someone's perspective. I don't expect them to run down to a sporting goods store, sign up on the forums, and show up at the next rally, but perhaps they won't react the same way the next time they see a peaceful law-abiding citizen with a gun.

Because I go through this frequently, I try to follow some basic rules when I'm OC'ing.

•   **Holster and Safety Measures:** My preference is to wear the holster for a cross-torso draw with my strong hand. In addition to being generally out of the way, it's impossible to grab from behind and an observer can see I have muzzle awareness and control of my gun. I check the placement of my holster and the safety on my gun whenever I enter or exit my vehicle, stand up, or sit down.

•   **Clean-cut appearance:** One of the things the military taught me was how to look presentable and represent the service in and out of uniform, on and off-post. To that end I try to do the same for the sake of the organization I'm involved in. I keep my hair short, my face clean-shaven, and my attire conservative. "Unkempt and armed" is not an image I want to present to the world.

•   **Familiarity with local laws:** Though my law notes contain general guidelines (and I work to expand it) it's important to be familiar with the laws in the area I'm OC'ing in. If there's something on the books, I need to be able to articulate why it violates state pre-emption. I need to know what signs a business should have posted if they are not gun-friendly, and who has the authority to ask me to leave. "I don't know" is not an acceptable answer, especially if I'm dealing with law enforcement or store security.

- **Justification beyond the law:** The questions aren't always legal. People sometimes ask *why* I would OC, and I like to have more to say than "it's my right" or "why shouldn't I?" If I'm in a position where I can have a longer conversation, I'll talk about the stages of violent crime and provide examples of ways that guns are used to prevent it.

- **Choosing my battles:** For some people, no justification will be sufficient. It's important to stop arguing your point before things get heated, "angry and armed" is a lot worse than "unkempt and armed." I don't want to be seen as someone drawing attention to himself, which is happening enough already without raising my voice.

- **Politeness:** Along the same lines as the last point, I make an effort not to be combative. If someone asks why I have a gun, "Why the heck shouldn't I?" is not an answer that helps anyone. Being "the grump with the gun" is almost the worst thing possible for the public image of open-carry.

- **One thing at a time:** The Second Amendment is not the only "issue" I'm involved in, though I would say it's the one I place the most emphasis on. But if I'm already drawing flak for something else, my gun is likely to make me the target of an off-topic *ad hominem* ("to the man") attack. I also don't want my personal beliefs to be conflated (merged) with the open-carry crowd as a whole.

- **Curb my enthusiasm:** I never drink and carry, even in my own home, and especially not in public. It's legal up to .08, but why in the world would I want alcohol on my breath and a gun on my hip? That's begging for trouble from law enforcement, establishment owners, and anyone else who crosses my path. I would consider "intoxicated and armed" the worst possible image an OC'er could present to the world.

These guidelines have served me well in the time since I stopped wearing my holster under my jacket. Your mileage may vary, of course, but generally speaking I feel that we can make a little difference every day by practicing the principles I've outlined in this list.

7
Why Open Carry Laws Work

By *John Pierce, cofounder of OpenCarry.org with an M.B.A. from George Mason University in Fairfax, Va.*

Second Amendment or not, law-abiding citizens have the right to go about their business.

• The phrase 'open carry' refers to the act of law-abiding citizens carrying a properly holstered handgun in plain sight, wherever it is legal to do so, as they go about their every day lives — such as driving to work, walking the dog, grabbing a cup of coffee at Starbucks, or buying a book at Barnes & Noble. Those who choose 'open carry' are just going about their business while armed, just as do the six-million-plus Americans who hold 'concealed carry' permits. The only difference — 'open carriers' have taken off their jackets.

Contrary to popular opinion, the ability to carry a weapon openly does not currently derive from the Second Amendment to the U.S. Constitution but rather from the constitutions and statutes of the 50 states. This is important because those who are opposed to 'open carry' often attempt to characterize it as an oddity of the law or a mischaracterization of the U.S. Constitution. Nothing could be farther from the truth.

In fact, in the majority of states, any law-abiding citizen who is not otherwise prohibited by law from possessing a firearm may openly carry a loaded handgun with no license or permit required. In the majority of these 29 states, this right is based upon state constitutional provisions. And while anti-gun activists often argue that the prefatory clause of the Second Amendment to the U.S. Constitution brings the intent of the framers into question, the history, tradition, and practice of law-abiding citizens peacefully bearing arms is spelled out time and time again in state constitutional provisions whose interpretation is clear.

In an additional 14 states, citizens who hold a state-issued carry permit may carry openly or concealed as they see fit. It is of particular import that in these states, the legislatures crafted their carry statutes in such a way as to avoid requiring concealment of the firearms thus carried. If open carry were the public safety issue that anti-gun activists proclaim it to be, it would be hard to imagine 14 separate legislatures actively passing legislation enabling the practice. It is also illustrative to note that the majority of these carry statutes have been passed within the last several decades. This demonstrates that such legislative thought is not an anachronism, as often claimed by those people who are anti-gun. Rather, such carry statutes reflect a modern, individual-rights focus that finds open carry appropriate when balancing the personal protection interests of its citizens with the state's interest in ordered liberty.

In attempting to discredit open carry, anti-gun activists often like to ask the question, "How do I know that the person openly carrying is in fact a law-abiding citizen and not a criminal?" While this is an attempt to imply that anyone who lawfully carries a firearm is a potential criminal, thankfully there is an authoritative answer available.

The 2006 FBI study *"Violent Encounters: A Study of Felonious Assaults on Our Nation's Law Enforcement Officers"*, by Anthony Pinizzotto, revealed that criminals carefully conceal their firearms, and they eschew the use of holsters. In layman's terms, this report tells us that, statistically speaking, citizens who are openly wearing a properly holstered handgun and are willing to subject themselves to the intense public and law enforcement scrutiny, that open carry brings with it, are not criminals.

But with open carry legal in some form in 43 states, and with the practice becoming increasingly common, it is not surprising that citizens unfamiliar with the practice might have questions when they first see a neighbor carrying openly. And these questions are often directed to local law enforcement. One of the key missions of this book is to serve as an educational resource for citizens and law enforcement alike when such questions arise in order to insure that interactions between citizens and law enforcement respect both the rights of the citizen and the difficult job being performed by the officer. Interestingly, the increasing normality of open carry has helped to ensure that law enforcement officers across the country have been educated about its legality, rendering such encounters infrequent.

So is open carry right for America? The answer is an unequivocal "yes!" Already present in the vast majority of states, the increasing popularity of the open-carry movement is a visible symbol that the right to bear arms remains a vital core right of American citizens.

Gun Carry In the USA

8
Open Carry Demonstrations & Events

- May 2, 1967, openly armed members of the Black Panther Party marched on the California State capitol in opposition to the Mulford Act prohibiting the public carrying of loaded firearms. The act had been prompted by the Panthers patrolling with shotguns.

- June 16, 2000, the New Black Panther Party along with the National Black United Front and the New Black Muslim Movement protested the death sentencing conviction of Gary Graham, by openly carrying shotguns and rifles at the Texas Republican National convention in Houston, Texas.

- In 2003, gun rights supporters in Ohio used a succession of Open Carry "Defense Walks" attempting to persuade the Governor to sign concealed carry legislation into law.

- The legality of open carry of certain firearms in Virginia was reaffirmed after several 2004 incidents in which citizens openly carrying firearms were confronted by local law enforcement. The Virginia law prohibits the open carry, in certain localities, of any semiautomatic weapon holding more than 20 rounds or a shotgun that holds more than seven rounds, without a concealed carry permit.

- In 2008, Clachelle and Kevin Jensen, of Utah, were photographed together openly carrying handguns in the Salt Lake City International Airport near a "no weapons" sign. The photo led to an article in *The Salt Lake Tribune* about the airport's preempted "no weapons" signs. After a few weeks, the city removed the unlawful signs.

• In 2008, Staff Sergeant Zachary Nelson Mead was detained in Richmond County, Georgia for openly carrying a firearm. The firearm was seized by Deputy Kadum Townsend. The organization GeorgiaCarry.org filed a lawsuit on behalf of Staff Sergeant Mead. The court declared that the seizure was a violation of the Fourth Amendment to the United States Constitution, awarded court costs and attorney fees to Mead, and dismissed the remaining charges with prejudice.

• In 2008, Brad Krause of West Allis, Wisconsin was arrested by police for alleged disorderly conduct while openly carrying a firearm while planting a tree on his property. A court later acquitted him of the disorderly conduct charge, observing in the process that in Wisconsin there is no law dealing with the issue of unconcealed weapons.

• On April 20, 2009, Wisconsin Attorney General J.B. Van Hollen issued a memorandum to district attorneys stating that open carry was legal and in and of itself does not warrant a charge of disorderly conduct. Milwaukee police chief Ed Flynn instructed his officers to take down anyone with a firearm, take the gun away, and then determine if the individual could legally carry it, until they could make sure the situation is safe.

• On May 31, 2009, Washington OpenCarry.org members held an open carry protest picnic at Silverdale's Waterfront Park, a county park. Attendees openly carried handguns in violation of posted regulations prohibiting firearms at the park. Kitsap county Sheriff's deputies were on hand, in part to explain to the public why they weren't enforcing the park's posted gun ban. Washington state law allows the open carrying of firearms and specifically preempts local ordinances more restrictive than the state's. Kitsap County has left its parks gun ban on the books and continues to publicly post it with other park regulations. Because the law is not practically enforceable, there has been confusion among gun owners as to whether open carry will be tolerated.

• In July 2009, an open carry event organized by OpenCarry.org took place at Pacific Beach, San Diego, California, where citizens carrying unloaded pistols and revolvers were subjected to Section 12031(e) inspections of their firearms on demand by police officers. The officers were obviously well-briefed on the details of the law, which allows Californians to openly carry only unloaded guns, but also allows carry of loaded magazines and speedloaders.

• On August 11, 2009, William Kostric, a New Hampshire resident, Free State Project participant, and former member of We The People's Arizona Chapter, was seen carrying a loaded handgun openly in a holster while participating in a rally outside a town hall meeting hosted by President Barack Obama at Portsmouth High School in New Hampshire. Kostric never attempted to enter the school, but rather stood some distance away on the private property of a nearby church, where he had permission to be. He held up a sign that read, "It's Time to Water the Tree of Liberty!"

• On August 16, 2009, "about a dozen" people were noted by police to be openly carrying firearms at a health care rally across the street from a Veterans of Foreign Wars Convention in the Phoenix Convention Center, where President Barack Obama was giving an address. While the Secret Service was "very much aware" of these individuals, Arizona law does not prohibit open carry. No crimes were committed by these protesters, and no arrests were made.

In an interview with Fox News, commentator James Wesley Rawles characterized the Phoenix protesters as "merely exercising a pre-existing right". When he was asked about open carry, "but...without a permit?" Rawles opined, "We *have* a permit — it is called the Second Amendment."

• On January 30, 2010, members of Michigan Open Carry were eating at a local Ponderosa Steakhouse in Lansing, Michigan, when the local police department came and forced the citizens to leave. A person rumored to be a United States Marine was carrying an AR-15 at this open carry event. A brief verbal discussion ensued between the leader of the open carry group and the Lansing Police Department. No arrests were made; some of the law enforcement officers at the scene were given reprimands for their actions arising from the incident.

9

Should I Carry A Gun?

By Norman Hamann

This is a question that many people may not give enough thought to. Carrying a firearm in your everyday life is a huge responsibility, and one that should not be taken lightly. I fully support the right of all citizens to bear arms in their day to day activities. However, I do believe that there are people, perhaps even *most* people, who should not choose to carry.

Allow me to explain.

The first question you should ask yourself is: *Can* I carry a gun? Do I know the laws that come into play when I carry? There are federal, state, and in many places, local laws that come into play when carrying firearms. I do not believe it is a responsible decision to just say, **"I have the Constitution of the United States, and it says that the right to bear arms shall not be infringed."**

Don't get me wrong, I agree with that interpretation of the Constitution. However, are you willing to go to jail for an extended period of time to argue that interpretation? If you are willing, I applaud your bravery and I wish you luck, but I guarantee it will be a long hard battle, and you have no assurance of a positive outcome. I suggest you study relevant law. Study it until you know it well enough to quote it when questioned, and follow it to the letter.

The next question you should ask yourself is, **"Am I responsible enough to carry a gun?"**

Many people in this country are not responsible enough to be trusted with a firearm in their possession. Do you plan on drinking alcohol while carrying? If you plan to, you probably should not carry. Are you forgetful? Forgetting a purse in a restaurant isn't all that bad. It can be replaced or recovered. But if you have a firearm in that purse and you forget it, now other people may have access to that firearm. Bad things can happen. A firearm is a dangerous weapon. Its ultimate function is to kill. It should always be treated with the respect and care it deserves.

The last question and perhaps the most important question you should ask yourself is, ***"Am I prepared to use my gun?"***

We all hate to think of the possibility of someday having to take a life to save our own life or the life of a loved one, but you must remember that *self protection is the whole reason you wanted to carry the gun in the first place.* Very few people have the mental fortitude to be able to take a life when it becomes necessary to save your own. Even soldiers in battle include an overwhelming number who will refuse to actually take a life and will shoot over the enemy's head in the actual moment of combat.

If you don't have the conviction to be able to protect yourself with a gun when the need arises, and if you choose to carry anyway, then all you have done is given the bad guy a weapon to take and use against you. I suggest that you make the responsible choice not to carry.

For those of you who answer in the affirmative to all of those questions and make the decision to carry a firearm, I suggest you jump in with both feet. Get a good, reliable and safe gun, get a good secure holster, get a strong secure belt, and always carry 100% of the time you are legally allowed to. Get training, both lethal and non-lethal. Get practice. Build your skills because you are one of the few defenses that people have, and if the moment comes, you'd best be as prepared as possible to handle the situation.

Gun Carry In the USA

10
The Bible and Self Defense

After a plea to Americans to buy firearms as a first step to fighting terrorism, a number of devoted Christians wrote and challenged this prescription as unbiblical, unscriptural and ungodly.

Wrong. The Bible couldn't be clearer on the right we have — even the *duty* we have as believers — to self-defense.

Let's start in the Old Testament.

"If a thief be found breaking [in], and be smitten that he die, there shall no blood be shed for him," — Exodus 22:2.

The next verse says:

"If the sun be risen upon him, there shall be blood shed for him; for he should make full restitution; if he have nothing, then he shall be sold for his theft."

In other words, it was OK to kill a thief breaking into your house if he could not be otherwise stopped. This is the ultimate expression of self-defense. It doesn't matter whether the thief is threatening your life or not; you have the right to protect your home, your family, and your property.

The Israelites were expected to have their own personal weapons. Every man would be summoned to arms when the nation was confronted by an enemy. They didn't depend on the Marines; the people defended themselves.

"And David said unto his men, Gird ye on every man his sword. And they girded on every man his sword;

and David also girded on his sword: and there went up after David about four hundred men; and two hundred abode by the stuff." — 1 Samuel 25:13.

Every man had a sword and every man picked it up when it was required.

Judges 5:8 reminds us of what happens to a foolish nation that chooses to disarm: *"They chose new gods; then was war in the gates: was there a shield or spear seen among forty thousand in Israel?"*

The answer to the rhetorical question is clear:

No! No shield nor spear was seen among the forty thousand in Israel. The people had rebelled against God and put away their weapons of self-defense.

"Blessed be the LORD my strength which teacheth my hands to war, and my fingers to fight," David writes in *Psalms 144:1.*

Clearly, this was not the pacifist God we serve. God teaches *"[our] hands to war and [our] fingers to fight."*

Over and over again throughout the Old Testament, His people are commanded to fight when threatened, with the best weapons available to them at that time.

And what were those weapons? Swords. They didn't have *firearms,* but they had *sidearms.* In fact, on the eve of his crucifixion, Jesus commanded His disciples to buy a sidearm and strap it on. Don't believe this? Check it out.

"And he said unto them, When I sent you without purse, and scrip, and shoes, lacked ye any thing? And they said Nothing.

"Then said he unto them, But now, he that hath a purse, let him take it, and likewise his scrip: and he that hath no sword, let him sell his garment, and buy one." — Luke 22:35,36.

I know. I know. You biblically literate skeptics are going to cite how Jesus responded when Peter used his sword to cut off the ear of a servant of the high priest:

"Then said Jesus unto him, Put up again thy sword into his place: for all they that take the sword shall perish with the sword. Thinkest thou that I cannot now pray to my Father, and he shall presently give me more than twelve legions of angels? But how then shall the scriptures be fulfilled, that thus it must be?" — Matthew 26:52-54.

Read those verses in context and they support the author's position.

Jesus told Peter that Peter would be committing suicide to decide to fight in this situation — undermining God's plan for Jesus to die on the cross and live again.

Jesus told Peter to put up his sword into its place at his side. He didn't say throw it away. After all, he had just ordered the disciples to arm themselves — to protect the lives of the disciples, not the life of the Son of God.

What Jesus was saying was: *"Peter, this is not the right time for a fight."*

In the context of America's current battle — after the devastation of Sept. 11, 2001 — as we made plans to rebuild and defend ourselves at the same time — we should recall Nehemiah, who rebuilt the walls of Jerusalem.

"They which builded on the wall, and they that bare burdens, with those that laded, every one with one of his hands wrought in the work, and with the other hand held a weapon." — Nehemiah 4:17-18.

"For the builders, every one had his sword girded by his side, and so builded."

Gun Carry In the USA

11
Minutemen

Minutemen were members of teams of select men from the American colonial partisan militia during the American Revolutionary War. They provided a highly mobile, rapidly deployed force that allowed the colonies to respond immediately to war threats, hence the name.

The minutemen were among the first people to fight in the American Revolution. Their teams made up about one-forth of the entire militia. Generally younger and more mobile, they served as part of a network for early response. Minuteman and Sons of Liberty member Paul Revere were among those who spread the news that the British Regulars (soldiers) were coming out from Boston. Revere was captured before completing his mission when the British marched toward the arsenal in Lexington and Concord to confiscate the weapons stored there.

The term has also been applied to various later United States civilian-based military forces to recall the success and patriotism of the originals.

Minutemen played a crucial role not only in the Revolutionary War, but in earlier conflicts.

Although the terms *militia* and *minutemen* are sometimes used interchangeably today, in the 18th century there was a decided difference between the two. Militia were men in arms formed to protect their towns from foreign invasion and ravages of war.

Minutemen were a small hand-picked elite force which were required to be highly mobile and able to assemble quickly.

Minutemen were selected from militia muster rolls by their commanding officers. Typically 25 years of age or younger, they were chosen for their enthusiasm, reliability, and physical strength. Usually about one quarter of the militia served as Minutemen, performing additional duties as such. The Minutemen were the first armed militia to arrive, or await a battle.

Although today Minutemen are thought of as connected to the Revolutionary War in America, their existence was conceived in Massachusetts during the mid-seventeenth century. As early as 1645, men were selected from the militia ranks to be dressed with matchlock rifles or pikes and equipment within half an hour of being warned.

In 1689 another type of Minuteman company came into existence. Called Snowshoemen, each was to "provide himself with a good pair of snowshoes, one pair of moccasins, and one hatchet" and to be ready to march on a moment's notice.

Minutemen also played a role in the French and Indian War in the 1750's. A journal entry from Samuel Thompson, a Massachusetts militia officer, states, "...but when our men were gone, they sent eleven more at one minute's warning, with 3 days provision..."

By the time of the Revolution, Minutemen had been a well-trained force for six generations in the Massachusetts Bay Colony. Every town had maintained its "training band". The adversity that this region faced — Native-American uprisings, war with France, and potential for local insurrections, social unrest, and rioting — provided ample reason to adhere to a sound militia organization.

David Hackett Fischer, author of *Paul Revere's Ride,* perhaps puts it best, **"The muster of the Minutemen in 1775 was the product of many years of institutional development...it was also the result of careful planning and collective effort."** By the time of the Revolution, Massachusetts had been training, drilling, and improving their militia for well over a hundred years.

Unfortunately, one thing the Minutemen lacked was central leadership. This disadvantage, among other things, would lead to their eventual dissolution.

In February of 1775, Concord was one of the first towns to comply with the order to create Minutemen companies out of the militia. Of approximately 400 militia from Concord's muster rolls, one hundred would also serve as Minutemen.

When a battle took place, Minutemen companies from several towns would combine their units. An officer from the 43rd Regiment of Foot was sent to the North Bridge in Concord with a number of light infantry. Minutemen from Concord, Acton, Littleton, and other Massachusetts towns, combined forces. After a few volleys were fired, the British light infantry retreated back to the Concord Common area.

Lacking central command, with each company of Minutemen loyal to their own town, they did not pursue the Redcoats. In the running battle that ensued, along the fifteen miles back to Boston the Massachusetts, militiamen would see their last action as Minutemen in history. The militia went on to form an army, surrounding Boston and inflicting heavy casualties on the British at Breed's and Bunker Hill.

Thus, although lacking central command, the Minutemen were still better organized and battle tested than any other part-time military. They were a vital and necessary force, playing a crucial role in not only the Revolutionary War, but in earlier conflicts. Without these **"ready in a minute"** men, our history may have been written in a very different way.

12
Equipment, Training & Tactics

Most Colonial militia units were provided neither with arms nor uniforms, and were required to equip themselves. Many simply wore their own farmers' or workmans' clothes, and in some cases they wore cloth hunting frocks. Most used fowling pieces, though rifles were sometimes used by men where rifles were available. Neither fowling pieces nor rifles had bayonets. Some colonies purchased muskets, cartridge boxes, and bayonets from England, and maintained armories within the colony.

The Continental Army regulars received European-style military training, later in the American Revolutionary War, but the militias did not get much of this. Rather than fight formal battles in the traditional dense lines and columns, they fought better when used as irregulars, primarily as skirmishers and sharpshooters. When used in conjunction with continental regulars, the militia would frequently fire ragged irregular volleys from a forward skirmish line, or the flanks of the Continental Army, while Continental soldiers held the center.

Their experience suited irregular warfare. Most were familiar with frontier hunting. The Indian Wars, and especially the recent French and Indian War, had taught both the men and officers the value of irregular warfare, while many English troops fresh from Europe were less familiar with this. The long rifle was also well suited to this role. The rifling (grooves inside the barrel) gave it a much greater range than the smoothbore musket, although it took much longer to load. Because of the lower rate of fire, rifles were not used by regular infantry, but were preferred for hunting.

When performing as skirmishers, the militia could fire and fall back behind cover, or other troops, before the British could get into range. The wilderness terrain that lay just beyond many colonial towns, very familiar to the local minuteman, favored this style of combat. In time, however, people like Rogers, Butler, and Simcoe, who remained loyal, mustered equally capable irregular forces. In addition, many British commanders learned from experience and effectively modified their light infantry tactics and battle dress to suit conditions in North America.

Through the remainder of the revolution, militias moved to adopting the minuteman model for rapid mobilization. With this rapid mustering of forces, the militia proved its value by serving as supporters to the continental army on a temporary basis occasionally leading to instances of numerical superiority. This was seen at the Battles of Hubbardston and Bennington in the north and at Camden and Cowpens in the south. Cowpens is notable in that Daniel Morgan used the militias' strengths and weaknesses skillfully to attain the double-envelopment of Tarleton's forces.

The historian M. L. Brown states that while a few of these men mastered the difficult handling of a rifle, few became expert. Brown quotes the Continental Army soldier Benjamin Thompson, who expressed the "common sentiment" at the time which was that minutemen were notoriously poor marksmen with rifles:

> Instead of being the best marksmen in the world and picking off every Regular that was to be seen...the

continual firing which they kept up by the week and the month has had no other effect than to waste their ammunition and convince the King's troops that they are really not really so formidable. — *Firearms in Colonial America: The Impact on History and Technology, 1492-1792, Page 306.*

Ammunition and supplies were in short supply and were constantly being seized by British patrols. As a precaution, these items were often hidden or left behind by minutemen in fields or wooded areas. Other popular concealment methods were to hide items underneath floorboards in houses and barns.

13
Big Brother

Big Brother is scared of people with guns, as all tyranni-cal and oppressive regimes have been in the past, because an armed population can resist a government aimed at destroying civil liberties or rounding up citizens and sending them to detention centers or death camps.

By disarming ordinary law abiding citizens, it also allows a government to grow in size and power because people would need to rely on the police to protect them from dangerous criminals, instead of protecting themselves using their own guns.

This allows the police force to grow larger and have more funding. Gun Control laws made it illegal for citizens to own guns that aren't registered to them, something that can easily allow officials to do door-to-door weapon confiscations like they did in the aftermath of hurricane Katrina in 2003. Police can pull up a person's name and instantly see which guns they own, and demand that they get turned in.

While New World Order kingpins continuously attempt to destroy the Second Amendment to the Constitution, there are other Orwellian policies being put into place in attempts to monitor who has what guns, and even how many bullets they own.

As governor of California, Arnold Schwarzenegger signed a bill into law which required stores that sell ammu-nition to thumbprint customers and log their driver's license for each purchase. Everyone who now buys bullets in California must submit to the procedure, as well as sign for their purchase which is then entered into a federal database that keeps track of how much ammo that person has bought.

The database is used to flag people who buy what Big Brother considers large amounts of ammunition, which may then be considered probable cause to investigate the individual further or place them under surveillance.

Schwarzenegger claimed to be against such a policy in the past but later changed his mind saying, "Although I have previously vetoed legislation similar to this measure, local governments have demonstrated that requiring ammunition vendors to keep records on ammunition sales improves public safety."

Sam Peredes, the executive director of Gun Owners of California, said that the law treats gunowners like registered sex offenders.

14
Orwellian Government Programs

While the "alphabet agencies" (CIA, NSA, FBI, ATFE, etc.) have access to incredible Big Brother technology and countless commercial and government databases, there are also creepy Orwellian projects that have been secretly created and funded by elements within the government for the purpose of maintaining the power of the ruling elite.

Many of these programs used (and continue to use) underhanded and often illegal methods to accomplish their goals which range from controlling the mainstream media to covertly trying to smear, intimidate, blackmail, or even assassinate people who pose a threat to the establishment.

Often Orwellian goals are defended by the government claiming that such measures are needed to keep people safe from criminals or terrorists, but it is often the very people working for these programs who are the criminals.

Immediately after the September 11th attacks of 2001, the government fear-mongering began and was used as a justification for subverting the Constitution of the United States and implementing the long-awaited Orwellian dreams of the establishment. Any resistance to the new tyrannical, invasive, and unconstitutional measures is attacked as being unpatriotic. Officials continuously say that we needed to give up some of our freedoms in order to keep people safe from terrorists, which were said to lurk around every corner.

Thomas Jefferson famously stated, *"Those who would give up essential liberty to purchase a little temporary safety deserve neither liberty nor safety."* Jefferson obviously knew the strategy of tyrannical leaders and how they use fear-mongering as a justification to increase their power and trample over the population.

We must actively counter propaganda and lies, and hold corrupt government officials accountable for their crimes. Only an educated and alert public can counter the invisible empire and their Orwellian dreams. We must use the tools of advanced technology to enhance and simplify the human experience, not to stifle nor destroy it.

We must stay strong in the face of immense opposition and remember what Martin Luther King Jr. said when he proclaimed, *"He who passively accepts evil is as much involved in it as he who helps to perpetrate it. He who accepts evil without protesting against it is really cooperating with it."*

We outnumber the elite Illuminati thousands to one, and if we can awaken our fellow man to see the system we are all victims of, and if we can lift the veil of ignorance and apathy we can unite and restore our communities, our country, and the world with the inalienable rights with which we have been endowed by our Creator.

We know that Big Brother is watching us, so let's show him what we are peacefully capable of.

15

What About Gun Control?

By Larry Pratt - *Executive Director of Gun Owners of America.*

The underlying argument for gun control seems to be that the availability of guns causes crime. By extension, the availability of *any* weapon would have to be viewed as a cause of crime. What does the Bible say about such a view?

Perhaps we should start at the beginning, or at least very close to the beginning. In Genesis 4, we read about the first murder. Cain had offered an unacceptable sacrifice, and Cain was upset that God insisted that he do the right thing.

In other words, Cain was peeved that he could not do his thing his own way. Cain decided to kill his brother rather than get right with God. There was no gun available, although there may well have been a knife.

Whether it was a knife or a rock, the Bible does not say. The point is, that the evil in Cain's heart was the cause of the murder, not the availability of the murder weapon.

God's response was not to ban rocks or knives, or whatever, but to banish the murderer. Later God instituted capital punishment (see Genesis 9:5-6) but said nothing about banning weapons.

Did Christ Teach Pacifism? Many people, Christians included, assume that Christ taught pacifism. They cite Matthew 5:38,39 for their proof.

"Ye have heard that is was said, 'An eye for an eye, a tooth for a tooth, But I tell you not to resist an evil person. But whoever slaps you on your right cheek, turn the other to him also," i.e., go the second mile; *do not take revenge.*

The Sermon on the Mount from which this passage is taken deals with righteous personal conduct. Here, Jesus is clearing up a confusion that had led the people to think that conduct proper for the civil government — taking vengeance – was also proper for an individual.

Even the choice of words Jesus used indicates that he was addressing a commonplace confusion, or distortion. Several times in the rest of the Sermon on the Mount Jesus used this same *"you have heard it said"* figure of speech to straighten out misunderstandings or falsehoods being taught by the religious leaders of the times.

Contrast this to Jesus's use of the phrase *"it is written"* when He was appealing to the Scriptures for authority. *For example, see Matthew 4 where on three occasions during His temptation by the devil, Christ answered each one of the devil's lies or misquotes from the Scripture with the words: "it is written".*

To further underscore the point that Jesus was correcting the religious leaders on their teaching that *"an eye for an eye"* applies to *private revenge,* consider that in the same Sermon, Jesus strongly condemned false teaching:

"Whoever therefore breaks one of the command-ments, and teaches men so, shall be called least in the kingdom of heaven..." — Matthew 5:19.

Clearly, then, Jesus was not teaching anything different about self defense than is taught elsewhere in the Bible. If otherwise, he would be contradicting himself for he would be teaching men to break one of the commandments. The Bible distinguishes clearly between the duties the individual.

Namely, that God has delegated to the Civil Magistrate the administration of justice, and to Individuals the responsibility of protecting there lives from attackers. Jesus was referring to this distinction in the Matthew 5 passage.

Let us now examine in some detail what the Scriptures say about the roles of government, and of individuals. Both the Old and New Testaments teach individual self defense, even if it means taking the assailant's life in certain circumstances.

Self Defense in the Old Testament tells us, at Exodus 22:2,3, *"If the thief is found breaking in, and he is struck so that he dies, there shall be no guilt for his bloodshed. If the sun has risen on him, there shall be guilt for his bloodshed. He should make full restitution; if he has nothing, then he shall be sold for his theft."*

One conclusion which can be drawn from this is that a threat to one's life is to be met with lethal force. During the day, presumably because we can recognize and later apprehend the thief if he escapes, we are not to kill under non life-threatening circumstances.

Not from the Bible but it follows the same line of thinking.

The Gun is Civilization by Maj. L. Caudill USMC (Ret).
Human beings have only two ways to deal with one another: *reason or force.* If you want me to do something for you, you have the choice of either convincing me via argument, or forcing me to do your bidding under threat of force.

Every human interaction falls into either one of those two categories, without exception. Reason or force, that's it.

In a truly moral and civilized society, people interact exclusively through persuasion. Force has no place as a valid method of social interaction in such a case. But the only thing that *removes force from the menu* is the personal firearm — *as paradoxical as this may sound to some.*

When I carry a gun, you cannot deal with me by force. You have to use reason and try to persuade me because I have a way to negate your threat or employment of force.

The gun is the only personal weapon that puts a 100-pound woman on equal footing with a 220-pound mugger, a 75-year old retiree on equal footing with a 19-year old gangbanger, and a single guy on equal footing with a carload of drunk guys with baseball bats.

The gun removes the disparity in physical strength, size or numbers between a potential attacker and a defender.

There are plenty of people who consider the gun as the source of more crimes. These are the people who think that we'd be more civilized if *all* guns were removed from society because our lack of a firearm would make it easier for an armed mugger to do his job.

This of course is only true if the mugger's potential victim is disarmed, either by choice or by legislative fiat; it has no validity when a mugger's potential mark is armed.

People who argue for the banning of arms ask for automatic rule by the young, the strong, and the many, which is the exact opposite of a civilized society. A mugger, even an armed one, can only make a successful living in a society where the state has granted him a monopoly on force.

Then there's the argument that the gun makes confrontations lethal that otherwise would only result in injury. This argument is fallacious in several ways. Without guns involved, confrontations are won by the physically superior party inflicting overwhelming injury on the loser.

People who believe that fists, bats, sticks, or stones don't constitute lethal force watch too much TV, where people take beatings and come out of it with bloody lips at the worst.

The fact that the gun makes lethal counter-force easier works in favor of the weaker defender, not the stronger attacker. Where both are armed the field is level.

The gun is the only weapon that is as lethal in the hands of an octogenarian as it is in the hands of a weight lifter. It wouldn't work as well as a force equalizer if it were not both lethal and easily employable.

When I carry a gun, I do not do so because I am looking for a fight. I'm looking to be left alone. The gun at my side means that I cannot be forced, only persuaded. I don't carry the gun because I'm afraid. It helps me to be unafraid and prepared.

It doesn't limit the actions of those who would interact with me through reason, only the actions of those who would do so by force. It removes force from the equation. That's why carrying a gun is a civilized act.

By Maj. L. Caudill USM C (Ret).

The greatest civilization is one where all citizens are equally armed and can only be persuaded by reason — never by force.

16
Columbine Father's Testimony

Guess our national leaders didn't expect this, hmm?

On Thursday, Darrell Scott, the father of Rachel Scott, a victim of the Columbine High School shootings in Littleton, Colorado, was invited to address the House Judiciary Committee's subcommittee. What he said to our national leaders during this special session of Congress was painfully truthful

They were not prepared for what he was to say, nor was it received well. It needs to be heard by every parent, every teacher, every politician, every sociologist, every psychologist, and every so-called expert! These courageous words spoken by Darrell Scott are powerful, penetrating, and deeply personal. There is no doubt that God sent this man as a voice crying in the wilderness. The following is a portion of the transcript:

"Since the dawn of creation there has been both good & evil in the hearts of men and women. We all contain the seeds of kindness or the seeds of violence. The death of my wonderful daughter, Rachel Joy Scott, and the deaths of that heroic teacher, and the other eleven children who died must not be in vain. Their blood cries out for answers.

"The first recorded act of violence was when Cain slew his brother Abel out in the field. The villain was not the club he used. Neither was it the NCA, the National Club Association. The true killer was Cain, and the reason for the murder could only be found in Cain's heart.

"In the days that followed the Columbine tragedy, I was amazed at how quickly fingers began to be pointed at groups such as the NRA. I am not a member of the NRA. I am not a hunter. I do not even own a gun. I am not here to represent or defend the NRA - because I don't believe that they are responsible for my daughter's death. Therefore I do not believe that they need to be defended. If I believed they had anything to do with Rachel's murder I would be their strongest opponent.

I am here today to declare that Columbine was not just a tragedy — it was a spiritual event that should be forcing us to look at where the real blame lies! Much of the blame lies here in this room. Much of the blame lies behind the pointing fingers of the accusers themselves. I wrote a poem just four nights ago that expresses my feelings best. This was written way before I knew I would be speaking here today:

Your laws ignore our deepest needs,
   Your words are empty air.
You've stripped away our heritage,
   You've outlawed simple prayer.
Now gunshots fill our classrooms,
   And precious children die.
You seek for answers everywhere,
   And ask the question "Why?"
You regulate restrictive laws,
   Through legislative creed.
And yet you fail to understand,
   That God is what we need!

"Men and women are three-part beings. We all consist of body, mind, and spirit. When we refuse to acknowledge a third part of our make-up, we create a void that allows evil, prejudice, and hatred to rush in and wreak havoc. Spiritual presences were present within our educational systems for most of our nation's history. Many of our major colleges began as theological seminaries. This is a historical fact. What has happened to us as a nation? We have refused to honor God, and in so doing, we open the doors to hatred and violence. And when something as terrible as Columbine's tragedy occurs — politicians immediately look for a scapegoat such as the NRA. They immediately seek to pass more restrictive laws that contribute to erode away our personal and private liberties. We do not need more restrictive laws. Eric and Dylan would not have been stopped by metal detectors. No amount of gun laws can stop someone who spends months planning this type of massacre. The real villain lies within our own hearts.

"As my son Craig lay under that table in the school library and saw his two friends murdered before his very eyes, he did not hesitate to pray in school. I defy any law or politician to deny him that right! I challenge every young person in America, and around the world, to realize that on April 20, 1999, at Columbine High School prayer was brought back to our schools. Do not let the many prayers offered by those students be in vain. Dare to move into the new millennium with a sacred disregard for legislation that violates your God-given right to communicate with Him. To those of you who would point your finger at the NRA — I give to you a sincere challenge. Dare to examine your own heart before casting the first stone!

My daughter's death will not be in vain! The young people of this country will not allow that to happen!"

Gun Carry In the USA

17

Gun Control Laws

Gun Control Laws

Gun control laws set the stage for genocide in the 20th century. A chart shows almost 56,00,000 victims of genocide in Seven different periods including the Nazi holocaust. The breakdown is as follows:

1. The Soviet Union established gun control in 1929; and from 1929 to 1953, 20 million political dissidents, unable to defend themselves, were rounded up and exterminated.

2. Turkey established gun control in 1911; and from 1915 to 1917, 1.5 million Americans, unable to defend themselves, were rounded up and exterminated.

3. Germany established gun control in 1928; and from 1939 to 1945, 13 million Jews, Gypsies, homosexuals, mentally ill people, the elderly, and other "mongrelized peoples," unable to defend themselves, were rounded up and exterminated.

4. China established gun control in 1935; and from 1948 to 1952, 20 million political dissidents, unable to defend themselves, were rounded up and exterminated.

5. Guatemala established gun control in 1964; and from 1964 to 1981 100,000 Mayan Indians, unable to defend themselves, were rounded up and exterminated.

6. Uganda established gun control in 1970; and from 1971 to 1979, 300,000 defenseless Christians were rounded up and exterminated.

7. Cambodia established gun control in 1956; and from 1975 to 1977, 1 million "educated people," unable to defend themselves, were rounded up and exterminated.

Afghanistan, however, had no gun control laws; and when the Soviets invaded Afghanistan in December of 1979, the citizens of Afghanistan were able to stymie and withstand the entire Soviet threat because the citizens were armed with military rifles and equipment. In 1989, the Soviets had enough and withdrew, licking their wounds.

— Article, *Jews of the Preservation of Firearms,* by Jay Sitrekin.

A letter dated July 12, 1968, from Lewis C. Coffin (*Law Librarian at the Library of Congress*), containing a copy of Hitler's **1938 Gun Control Act,** was sent to Senator Tom Dodd (*who had participated in the Nuremburg Trials in Berlin, Germany*), four months before the congressional subcommittee of which he was chairman presented the **1968 Gun Control Act** to Congress for passage. When placed side by side, the two laws read almost word for word in many of their sections.

18
The World Situation Today

Written by a retired attorney, to his sons.

Our country is now facing a most serious threat to its existence, as we know it, that we have faced in your lifetime and mine (which includes WW II). The deadly seriousness is greatly compounded by the fact that there are a very few of us who think we can possibly lose this war and even fewer who realize what losing really means.

First, let's examine a few basics:

1. When did the threat to us first seem to begin?

. . . Many will say September 11, 2001. One answer, as far as the United States is concerned, is 1979, 22 years prior to September 2001, with the following attacks on the United States:

• Iran Embassy Hostages, 1979;
• Beirut, Lebanon Embassy, 1983;
• Beirut, Lebanon Marine Barracks, 1983;
• Lockerbie, Scotland Pan-Am flight to New York, 1988;
• First New York World Trade Center attack, 1993;
• Dhahran, Saudi Arabia Khobar Towers Military complex, 1996
• Nairobi, Kenya US Embassy, 1998;
• Dares Salaam, Tanzania US Embassy, 1998;
• Aden, Yemen USS Cole, 2000;
• New York World Trade Center, 2001;
• The Pentagon, 2001.

(During the period from 1981 to 2001 there were 7,581 terrorist attacks worldwide.)

2. Why were we attacked?

. . . Envy of our position, our success, and our freedoms. The attacks happened during the administrations of Presidents Carter, Reagan, Bush Sr., Clinton and Bush Jr. We cannot fault either the Republicans or Democrats, as there were no provocations by any of the presidents or their immediate predecessor, President Ford.

3. Who were the attackers?

. . . In each case, the attacks on the U.S. were carried out by Muslims.

4. What is the Muslim population of the World?

. . . 25%.

5. Isn't the Muslim Religion peaceful?

. . . Hopefully, but that is really immaterial.

There is no doubt that the predominately Christian population of Germany was peaceful, but under the dictatorial leadership of Hitler (who claimed to be a Christian) that made no difference. You either went along with the administration in power or you were eliminated. There were 5 to 6 million Christians killed by the Nazis for political reasons (including 7,000 Polish priests).

Thus, almost the same number of Christians were killed by the Nazis as the six million holocaust Jews who were killed by them, and we seldom hear of anything other than the Jewish atrocities.

Although Hitler kept the world focused on the Jews, he did not hesitate to kill anyone who got in the way of his extermination of the Jews or his taking over of the world - be they German, Christian, or any others.

The same applies to the Muslim terrorists. They focus

the world on the United States but kill everyone in the way — be they their own people or the Spanish, British, French or anyone else. The point here is that just as the peaceful Germans were of no protection to anyone from the Nazis, no matter how many peaceful Muslims there may be they are no protection for us from the terrorist Muslim Leaders and what they are fanatically bent on doing — by their own pronouncements: killing all of us 'infidels'. I don't blame the peaceful Muslims. What would *you* do if your choice was to remain silent or be killed?

6. So who are we at war with?

. . . There is no way we can honestly tell that it is anyone other than the Muslim terrorists. Trying to be politically correct and avoid speaking of this conclusion can well be fatal. There is no way to win if you don't clearly recognize and articulate who is attacking you. So with that background, now come the two major questions . . . If we are to win, we must clearly answer these two pivotal questions:

1. Can we lose this war?
2. What does losing really mean?

We can definitely lose this war. And as anomalous as that may sound, the major reason we can lose this war is because so many of us simply do not fathom the answer to the second question — What does losing mean?

It appears as though a great many of us think that losing the war means simply hanging our heads, bringing the troops home, and going on about our business, like post-Vietnam. This is as far from the truth as one can get.

What losing really means is that we would no longer be the premier country in the world. The attacks would not subside, but would rather steadily increase. Remember, they want us dead; not just quiet. If they had just wanted us quiet, they would not have produced an increasing series of attacks against us over the past 32 years. The plan was, clearly, for terrorists to attack us until we were neutered and submissive to them.

We would of course have no future support from other nations for fear of reprisals and for the reason that they would see that we are impotent and cannot help them.

They will pick off the other non-Muslim nations one at a time. It will be increasingly easier for them. They already hold Spain hostage. It doesn't matter whether it was right or wrong for Spain to withdraw its troops from Iraq. Spain did it because the Muslim terrorists bombed their train and told them to withdraw the troops. Anything else they want Spain to do will be done. Spain is finished.

The next will probably be France. Our one hope with France is that they might see the light and realize that if we don't win they are finished, too, because they can't resist the Muslim terrorists without us. However, it may already be too late for France. France is already 20% Muslim and fading fast.

Without our support, Great Britain will go the way of France. Recently, I read that there are more Mosques in England than Churches.

If we lose the war, our production, income, exports, and way of life as we know it will all vanish. After losing, who would trade or deal with us if they were threatened by the Muslims? If we can't stop the Muslim terrorists, how could anyone else?

The radical Muslims fully know what is riding on this war, and therefore are completely committed to winning at any cost. We'd better know it, too, and be likewise committed to winning at any cost.

Why do I go on at such lengths about the results of losing?

. . . Simple. Until we recognize the costs of losing, we cannot unite and really put 100% of our thoughts and efforts into winning. And it is going to take that 100% effort to win.

So, how can we lose the war?

. . . Again, the answer is simple. We can lose the war by 'imploding. That is, defeating ourselves by refusing to recognize the enemy and their purpose and failing to dig in and lend full support to the war effort. If we are united, there is no way that we can lose. If we continue to be divided, there is no way that we can win.

Let me give you a few examples of how we simply don't comprehend the life and death seriousness of this situation: President Bush selects Norman Mineta as Secretary of Transportation. Although all of the terrorist attacks were committed by Muslim men between 17 and 40 years of age, Secretary Mineta refuses to allow profiling. Does that sound like we are taking this thing seriously? This is War!

For the duration, we are going to have to give up some of the civil rights to which we have become accustomed. We had better be prepared to lose some of our civil rights temporarily or we will most certainly lose all of them permanently. And don't worry that it is a slippery slope. We gave up plenty of civil rights during WW II, and immediately restored them after the victory ... and, in fact, added many more since that time.

Do I blame President Bush or President Clinton before him? No, I blame us for blithely assuming we can maintain all of our Political Correctness and all of our civil rights during this conflict and have a clean, lawful, honorable war. None of those words apply to war. Get them out of your head.

Some have gone so far in their criticism of the war and/or the Administration that it almost seems they would literally like to see us lose.

I think some actually do. I hasten to add that this isn't because they are disloyal. It is because they just don't recognize what losing means. Nevertheless, that conduct gives the impression to the enemy that we are divided and weakening. It concerns our friends and it does great damage to our cause.

Of more recent vintage, the uproar fueled by the politicians and media regarding the treatment of some prisoners of war perhaps exemplifies best what I am saying. We have recently had an issue involving the treatment of a few Muslim prisoners of war, by a small group of our military police.

These are the type of prisoners who just a few months ago were throwing their own people off buildings, cutting off their hands, cutting out their tongues, and otherwise murdering their own people just for disagreeing with Saddam Hussein.

And, just a few years ago, these same type of prisoners chemically killed 400,000 of their own people for the same reason. They are also the same type of enemy fighters who recently were burning Americans and dragging their charred corpses through the streets of Iraq. And, still more recently, the same type of enemy that was and is providing videos to all news sources internationally of the beheading alive by hand of American prisoners they held.

Compare this with some of our press and politicians, who

for several days have thought and talked about nothing else but the 'humiliating' of some Muslim prisoners — not burning them, not dragging their charred corpses through the streets, not beheading them, but 'humiliating' them. Can they be for real?

The politicians and pundits have even talked of impeachment of the Secretary of Defense. If this doesn't show the complete lack of comprehension and understanding of the seriousness of the enemy we are fighting, the life and death struggle we are in, and the disastrous results of losing this war, nothing can.

To bring our country to a virtual political standstill over this prisoner issue makes us look like Nero playing his fiddle as Rome burned — totally oblivious to what is going on in the real world. Neither we, nor any other country, can survive this internal strife. Again, I say, this does not mean that some of our politicians or media people are disloyal. It simply means that they are absolutely oblivious to the magnitude of the situation we are in and into which the Muslim terrorists have been pushing us for many years.

These people are a serious and dangerous liability to the war effort. We must take note of who they are and get them out of office. Remember, the Muslim terrorists stated goal is to kill all infidels. That translates into ALL non-Muslims — not just in the United States — but throughout the world. We are the last bastion of the world's defense.

We have been criticized for many years as being 'arrogant.' That charge is valid. We are arrogant in that we believe that we are so good, powerful, and smart that we can win the hearts and minds of all those who attack us, and that, with both hands tied behind our back, we can defeat anything bad in the world. We can't!

If we don't recognize this, our nation, as we know it, will not survive, and no other free country in the world will survive if we are defeated.

And, finally, name any Muslim countries throughout the world that allow freedom of speech, freedom of thought, freedom of religion, freedom of the press, equal rights for anyone — let alone everyone, equal status or any status for women, or that have been productive in one single way that contributes to the good of the world.

This has been a long way of saying that we must be united on this war or we will be equated in the history books to the self-inflicted fall of the Roman Empire. If, that is, the Muslim leaders will allow history books to be written or read.

If we don't win this war right now, keep a close eye on how the Muslims take over France in the next 5 years or less. They will continue to increase the Muslim population of France and continue to encroach, little by little, on the established French traditions.

The French will be fighting among themselves over what should or should not be done, which will continue to weaken them and keep them from any united resolve. Doesn't that sound eerily familiar?

Democracies don't have their freedoms taken away from them by some external military force. Instead, they give their freedoms away, politically correct piece by politically correct piece.

And they are giving those freedoms away to those who have shown, worldwide, that they abhor freedom and will not apply it to you or even to themselves, once they are in power.

Muslims have universally shown that when they have taken over, they then begin to brutally kill each other over which few will be controlling the masses.

What is happening in Iraq is a good example. Will we ever stop hearing from the politically correct about the 'peaceful Muslims'?

I close on a hopeful note by repeating what I said before: If we are united, there is no way that we can lose. I hope now, after the election, the factions in our country will begin to focus on the critical situation we are in, and will unite to save our country. It is your future we are talking about. Do whatever you can to preserve it. I reiterate: our national election is under way.

After reading the above, we all must do this, not only for ourselves, but for our children, our grandchildren, our country, and our world. Whether Democrat or Republican, conservative or liberal ... and that includes the Politicians and media of our country and the free world.

Please forward this to any you feel may want, or NEED to read it. Our 'leaders' in Congress ought to read it, too. There are those who find fault with our country, but it is obvious to anyone who truly thinks through this, that we must UNITE!

Lastly, I wish to add, at the risk of offending: I sincerely think that anyone who rejects this, as just another political rant, or doubts the seriousness of this issue, may be part of the problem.

We post this letter, hoping not to offend but to raise the awareness level of this world wide situation. It is time for plain speaking, plain thinking and decisive action!

We will never change the situation by pretending that it does not exist!

19

The Patriot Act

"The consciousness of being at war, and therefore in danger, makes the handing over of all power to a small caste seem the natural, unavoidable condition of survival." — George Orwell's, *Nineteen Eighty-Four.*

In response to the September 11th 2001 terrorist attacks on America, Congress quickly passed the PATRIOT ACT, which granted the government a wide range of unconstitutional powers so officials could allegedly prevent further terrorist attacks.

Any resistance to the bill was countered with claims that those people were un-American or wanted to help the terrorists. The very name for the bill, the "Patriot Act" was chosen to give the impression that if you were a patriotic American who loved his country, you would unquestionably support the bill.

The full title of the bill - "**U**nited and **S**trengthening **A**merica by **P**roviding **A**ppropriate **T**ools **R**equired to **I**ntercept and **O**bstruct **T**errorism **Act of 2001**" - was specifically designed to spell **USA PATRIOT Act**.

The only US Senator who voted against the bill, Russ Feingold of Wisconsin, did so because he saw that some of the provisions stripped away civil liberties guaranteed by the Constitution. He said:

"Of course there is no doubt that if we lived in a police state, it would be easier to catch terrorists. If we lived in a country that allowed the police to search your home at any time for any reason; if we lived in a country that allowed the government to open your mail, eavesdrop on your phone conversations, or intercept your e-mail communications; if we lived in a country that allowed the government to hold people in jail indefinitely based on what they write or think, or based on mere suspicion that they are up to no good, then the government would no doubt discover and arrest more terrorists. But that probably wouldn't be a country in which we would want to live."

The Bill is 343 pages long with 1,016 sections and amended more than 15 federal statutes, and contains numerous Executive Orders, regulations, and new policies aimed at "fighting terrorism". Many of these new powers allow the government to engage in secret surveillance and even commit "sneak and peeks" which mean that a person's house can be searched without his knowledge, while he is not served with a search warrant, or made aware that the search took place, until moths later.

If a neighbor happens to see a sneak and peak going on and is asking questions, then he can be placed under a gag order and be legally prevented from mentioning anything to anybody about what he saw.

The Patriot Act even allows for people to be detained for months without even being charged with a crime, a clear violation of the Sixth Amendment. In the first year after the Patriot Act was signed into law, more than 1,000 non citizens were secretly detained without being charged and their identities were not released. Thousands more were placed under government surveillance.

"In the vast majority of cases there was no trial, no report of the arrest. People simply disappeared." — George Orwell's, *Nineteen Eighty-Four.*

While everyone would agree that kidnapping, assassination or mass destruction would certainly be terrorism, intimidating the civilian population with coercion and intimidation, for attempting to influence government policy, could be applied to ordinary political rhetoric.

Critics of the Patriot Act claim that the Bush administration was guilty of intimidating the population by fabricating and exaggerating threats that led to the Iraq War. Others argue that the Patriot Act was a power grab by the government and that provisions were already in place to investigate and prevent terrorist attacks; and capture the perpetrators.

20

Federal Gun Free School Zones Act of 1995

The Federal Gun Free School Zone Act of 1995 severely limits where a person may legally carry a firearm by generally prohibiting carry within one-thousand (1000) feet of the **property-line** of any K-12 school in the nation with private property excluded. A State-issued permit to carry may exempt a person from this restriction depending on the laws of the particular State, and most issuing States qualify for this exception. However, according to BATFE (Bureau of Alcohol, Tobacco, Firearms and Explosives) the exception in Federal law is only applicable to permit holders while in the State that physically issued their permit, and does not exempt people with out-of-state permits, even when their permit is recognized through State reciprocity agreements.

Gun Carry In the USA

21
The Second Amendment

The Second Amendment, starting in the latter half of the 20th century, became an object of much debate. Concerned with rising violence in society and the role firearms play in that violence, gun control advocates began to read the Second Amendment one way. On the other side, firearm enthusiasts saw the attacks on gun ownership as attacks on freedom, and defended their interpretation of the Second Amendment just as fiercely. If the authors of the Second Amendment could have foreseen the debate, they might have phrased the amendment differently, because much of the debate has centered around the way the amendment is phrased.

Is the amendment one that was created to ensure the continuation and flourishing of the state militias as a means of defense, or was it created to ensure an individual's right to own a firearm?

Despite the rhetoric on both sides of the issue, the answer to both questions is most likely, "Yes."

The attitude of Americans toward the military was much different in the 1790's than it is today. Standing armies were mistrusted, as they had been used as tools of oppression by the monarchs of Europe for centuries. In the war for independence, there had been a regular army, but much of the fighting had been done by the state militias, under the command of local officers. Aside from the war, militias were needed because attacks were relatively common, whether by bandits, Indians, and even by troops from other states.

Today, the state militias have evolved into the National Guard in every state. These soldiers, while part-time, are professionally trained and armed by the government. No longer are regular, non-Guardsmen, expected to take up arms in defense of the state or the nation, though the US Code does still recognize the unorganized militia as an entity, and state laws vary on the subject. [see 10 USC 311].

This is in great contrast to the way things were at the time of adoption of the Second Amendment. Most state constitutions had a right to bear arms for the purposes of the maintenance of the militia. Many had laws that required men of age to own a gun and supplies, including powder and bullets.

In the state constitutions written around the time of the Declaration of Independence, the right to bear arms was presented in different ways. The Articles of Confederation specified that the states should maintain their militias, but did not mention a right to bear arms. Thus, any such protections would have to come from state law.

The Virginia Declaration of Rights, though it mentioned the militia, did not mention a right to bear arms — the right might be implied, since the state did not furnish weapons for militiamen. The constitutions of North Carolina and Massachusetts *did* guarantee the right, to ensure proper defense of the states.

The constitution of Pennsylvania guaranteed the right with no mention of the militia (at the time, Pennsylvania had no organized militia). One of the arguments of the Anti-Federalists during the ratification debates was that the new nation did not arm the militias, an odd argument since neither did the U.S. under the Articles of Confederation.

Finally, Madison's original proposal for the Bill of Rights

mentioned the individual right much more directly than the final result that came out of Congress.

Perhaps in the 1780's, the rise of a tyrant to a leadership position in the U.S. was a cause for concern. Today, the voters may have elected a leader whose stated aims might be to suppress freedom and declare martial law. For a leader whose unstated aim is to seize the nation, the task would be daunting. The size and scope of the conspiracy needed, the cooperation of patriots who would see right through such a plan — is unfathomable.

Many fear the rise in executive power under the Obama presidency is just such a usurpation, and in some ways it may be. But similar usurpations of power by the Congress and the President — such as the Alien and Sedition Acts, the suspension of habeas corpus during the Civil War, or the internment of Japanese-Americans during World War II — were all eventually overturned or struck down and then condemned by history. Our hope is that history will be our guide this time, too.

The defense of our borders had not been a cause for concern for nearly a century before the subject really came up again around the time of the turn of the millennium, in 1999. Concern with border defense became an an even greater issue after September 11, 2001, when a series of terrorist attacks, both in the form of hijacked airliners crashing into buildings and anthrax-laced mail, made people realize that we do have enemies that wish to invade our nation, though not on the scale of an army.

But while each state has its National Guard it can call up, the coordination is much more on a national scale, and special units of the regular army or border patrol are claimed to be better suited for such duty than the Guard.

Today's debate

These interpretations tend to lean in one of two ways. The first is that the amendment was meant to ensure that individuals have the absolute right to own firearms; the second is that the amendment was meant to ensure that States could form, arm, and maintain their own militias.

Either way, it is a bar to federal action only, because the Second Amendment has not been incorporated by the Supreme Court to apply to the states. This means that within its own constitution, a state may be as restrictive or non-restrictive as it wishes to be in the regulation of firearms; likewise, private rules and regulations may prohibit or encourage firearms. For example, if a housing association wishes to bar any firearm from being held within its borders, it is free to do so.

The Supreme Court, in permitting the United States to apply a stamp tax to sawed-off shotguns (a move, it was argued, that was intended to make such weapons *de factorially* illegal), essentially said that if a weapon does not contribute to the maintenance of a militia, and has no use in ensuring the common defense, it can be regulated (*United States v. Miller*, 307 US 174 [1939]).

Though the outcome of *Miller* was never fully resolved (the Court asked that Miller prove the relevance of the sawed-off shotgun to the maintenance of the militia, but Jack Miller died before he could, and the case died with him), the rationale used in *Miller* has been the basis for all gun control laws since 1939. As the GPO page notes, "At what point regulation or prohibition of what classes of firearms would conflict with the Amendment, if at all, the *Miller* case does little more than cast a faint degree of illumination toward an answer."

Both contemporary interpretations are correct, in a way.

As illustrated in the first section, the amendment does appear to have been designed to protect the militias, and it was also designed to protect an individual's right to own and bear a gun.

The question, then, is do we have to adhere to both tenets of the amendment today? If we decide to do away with the individual ownership aspect of the Amendment, reinterpreting the amendment to allow highly restricted gun ownership, we seem to open the door to radical reinterpretation of other, more basic parts of the Constitution. If we decide to do nothing, and allow unrestricted gun ownership, we run the risk of creating a society of the gun, a risk that we might not want to take. So the real question seems to be, can we have the a constitutional freedom to bear arms, and still allow some restriction and regulation?

Reasonable restrictions seemed to be the way to go, acknowledging the Amendment, but molding it, as we've done with much of the Constitution. After all, we have freedom of speech in the United States, but you are not truly free to say whatever you wish. You cannot incite violence without consequence; you cannot libel someone without consequence; you cannot shout "Fire!" in a crowded theater without consequence.

Why should not gun ownership be similarly regulated as it has been without violating the Constitution? Of course, prosecutions for gun ownership violations only take place after the fact — prosecutions of speech violations are no different.

The trick is finding that balance between freedom and reasonable regulation, between unreasonable unfettered ownership and unreasonable prior restraint. Gun ownership is indeed a right — but it is also a grand responsibility. With responsibility comes the interests of society to ensure that guns are used safely and are used by those with proper training and licensing. If we can agree on this simple premise, it should not be too difficult to work out proper compromise.

Recent developments

In 2007, the United States Court of Appeals for the District of Columbia Circuit ruled in the case of *Parker v District of Columbia*. In this case, the court ruled that D.C. laws which essentially prohibit the private ownership of handguns within the District, are unconstitutional. Specifically, the appellants, residents of D.C., were denied their Second Amendment rights by laws that bar the registration of handguns by anyone except retired D.C. police officers; that bar the carrying of a pistol without a license, even within one's home; and that require that lawfully owned firearms be kept unloaded and disassembled unless used for "lawful recreational purposes."

The Court found that in spite of the first part of the Second Amendment — that which refers to the militia — "the Second Amendment's premise is that guns would be kept by citizens for self-protection (as well as hunting)." The court acknowledged the history the militia played in the creation of the Second Amendment, but did not allow the militia to be sole measure to be viewed when looking at these laws restricting gun ownership and reasonable use. *Parker,* the court ruled, should be allowed to keep handguns in his home.

The case, filed as *District of Columbia v Heller*, was granted certiorari (*an order directing a lower court to deliver the record for review*) by the United States Supreme

Court, and was heard in March, 2008.

At issue were two questions. The first, raised by the District, is *whether the District is forbidden by the Second Amendment to ban the possession of handguns while allowing the possession of rifles and shotguns.* The second, broader issue is raised by Heller (another of the original petitioners in the Parker case): *whether the Second guarantees that guns, including handguns, can be kept in homes by law-abiding citizens.*

The Court decided that the issue it should hear is *"Whether the [D.C. laws] violate the Second Amendment rights of individuals who are not affiliated with any state-regulated militia, but who wish to keep handguns and other firearms for private use in their homes?"*

The Supreme Court ruled on the *Heller* case at the end of its term in June, 2008. The Court found for *Heller* in a close 5-4 decision *that the Second Amendment did, in fact, protect an individual right.*

While the court was careful to note that the case did not call into question any laws that regulate guns, it did state, unequivocally, that *Heller* and his fellow petitioners had a right to own guns in their home. The Court also ruled that while reasonable regulation may be permitted, *the requirement that guns be locked and disassembled was not reasonable.* The Court finally noted *that its ruling affected only the District of Columbia, as a federal enclave.*

Another case wss decided by the Court in 2010. In *McDonald v Chicago*, the constitutionality of restrictive local and state gun control laws was challenged. The case specifically challenged four limits placed on handgun registration by the city of Chicago and a suburb, Oak Park - *a ban on the registration of handguns; that all guns must be*

*registered prior to purchase; that all guns must be reregis-
tered annually; and that any lapse in a gun's registration
renders the gun permanently unregisterable.*

The plaintiffs in the case asked the Court to not only ren-
der the regulations unconstitutional, but to overrule the rule
of *selective incorporation* the Court has used since the late
1800's.

The Court ruled that the Chicago regulations were unconstitutional, and that *the rights previously found in the
Heller case were individual rights that also applied to state
and local governments.*

Justice Samuel Alito, writing for the majority, was matter-
of-fact in his conclusion:

"In *Heller*, we held that the Second Amendment protects
the right to possess a handgun in the home for the purpose
of self-defense. Unless considerations of stare decisis coun-
sel otherwise, a provision of the Bill of Rights that protects a
right that is fundamental from an American perspective applies equally to the Federal Government and the States. We
therefore hold that the Due Process Clause of the Fourteenth
Amendment incorporates the Second Amendment right recognized in *Heller*."

The Court refused, however, to abandon *the selective
incorporation process*. It also refused to remove all gun restrictions, recognizing that some, such as restrictions against
felons and the mentally ill and geographical restrictions, were
constitutional.

22

After Arizona Shooting Gun Control Advocates Push For New Restrictions

By Michael Beckel, *January 11, 2011.*

In the debate about Second Amendment rights and gun control, one side — gun supporters — typically has the upper hand. Now, gun control advocates are hoping momentum will build for new laws after the assassination attempt against Rep. Gabrielle Giffords (D-Ariz.) on Saturday in Tucson.

The weapon involved in the shooting was a Glock 19, a variation of a gun standard in many law enforcement departments.

Instead of the standard-issue 15 bullets in the magazine clip, the semi-automatic pistol was reportedly equipped with an extended magazine that could store 30 rounds of ammunition. The alleged shooter, 22-year-old Jared Lee Loughner, was jumped and restrained while trying to reload.

That type of ammunition clip increasingly looks to be the focus of a new legislative push for stricter regulations.

"People are completely outraged that there is a high-capacity magazine attached to a Glock," Josh Horwitz, the executive director of the Coalition to Stop Gun Violence, told *OpenSecrets Blog.* "These are offensive weapons," Horwitz continued. "We need to de-escalate... 30 rounds is a long time to wait for someone to reload."

But John Velleco, the director of federal affairs for the Gun Owners of America, told *OpenSecrets Blog* that lawmakers shouldn't jump to conclusions. He urged caution in lawmakers developing new regulations.

"Authorities don't know all the facts and already politicians like [New York Democratic Rep. Carolyn] McCarthy are blaming the 2nd Amendment, the Tea Party and far right for the actions of a confused and deranged young man," Velleco said.

"There is nothing to suggest that more gun control laws would have prevented this," he continued. "You can't just pass a law every time something bad happens and expect that to solve the problem."

On Monday, Rep. Carolyn McCarthy (D-N.Y.) — whose husband died during a 1993 mass shooting on the Long Island railroad — and Sen. Frank Lautenberg (D-N.J.) began drafting legislation to ban high-capacity ammunition magazines.

Such equipment was banned for a decade in the United States after President Bill Clinton in 1994 signed the Violent Crime Control and Law Enforcement Act into law. But the prohibition was designed to expire in 2004, and Congress did not renew it.

Another gun control advocate in Congress, Rep. Pete King (R-N.Y.), announced his plans to introduce legislation banning a person from bringing a gun within 1,000 feet of government officials, including the president, vice president, members of Congress and federal judges.

(Ed., the question is: "Would someone intent on killing obey such a legislated rule?")

23
Maine Gun Carry Laws

Maine State Constitution regarding the right to bear arms:

Section 16. To keep and bear arms. Every citizen has a right to keep and bear arms and this right shall never be questioned.

Maine State pre-emption over local codes:

Title 25, Part 5, Chapter 252-A of the Maine Revised Statutes establishes state pre-emption over local firearm codes.

§2011. State preemption

1. Preemption. The State intends to occupy and preempt the entire field of legislation concerning the regulation of firearms, components, ammunition and supplies. Except as provided in subsection 3, any existing or future order, ordinance, rule or regulation in this field of any political subdivision of the State is void.

[1989, c. 359, (NEW) .]

2. Regulation restricted. Except as provided in subsection 3, no political subdivision of the State, including, but not limited to, municipalities, counties, townships and village corporations, may adopt any order, ordinance, rule or regulation concerning the sale, purchase, purchase delay, transfer, ownership, use, possession, bearing, transportation, licensing, permitting, registration, taxation or any other matter pertaining to firearms, components, ammunition or supplies.

[1989, c. 359, (NEW) .]

3. Exception. This section does not prohibit an order, ordinance, rule or regulation of any political subdivision which, with the exception of appropriate civil penalty provisions, conforms exactly with any applicable provision of state law or which regulates the discharge of firearms within a jurisdiction.

[1989, c. 359, (NEW) .]

4. Law enforcement agency. Nothing in this section limits the power of any law enforcement agency to regulate the type and use of firearms issued or authorized by that agency for use by its employees. For the purposes of this section "law enforcement agency" has the same meaning as set forth in section 3701.

[1989, c. 502, Pt. D, §19 (NEW) .]

SECTION HISTORY

1989, c. 359, (NEW). 1989, c. 502, §D19 (AMD).

A summary of Maine firearm laws is available as a fact sheet in PDF file format from the National Rifle Association Institute for Legislative Action. (See http://tinyurl.com/ztlgz)

Generally speaking, OC is legal where there exists no standing state or federal precedent against it. In the absence of a legal ruling on the matter, OC is legal. When in doubt, ask your lawyer **before** you open-carry.

Examples of no-carry areas include:

- Post Offices
- USVA Togus
- Other Federal Buildings not listed, as well as Federal "facilities" owned, leased, or occupied by them
- State and Federal Courts, Jails, and Prisons
- K-12 School Zones (CC is legal with a valid Maine CFP)
- College Campuses
- Child Care Facilities, Nursery Schools and Foster Homes
- TSA-Secured areas of Airports
- Locations where there is a labor dispute or picket line (MRS Title 26, Chapter 7, Subchapter 1, Paragraph 5)
- Any business or establishment which posts a no-weapons policy, or on the request of the management of any such business or establishment.
- Locations with slot machines
- State Parks from May to September
- Acadia National Park (CC ok with a permit)

Additionally, it is illegal to possess a loaded firearm in a vehicle **unless** you posses a valid Maine or out of state (with reciprocity) CFP.

Concealed Carry is prohibited without a permit.

24
Frequently Asked Questions

1. Isn't protecting gun rights the NRA's job?

The National Rifle Association has a long history of defending firearm rights in the United States at both the state and federal level. However, as a large national organization they have a very broad scope of operation and many demands placed upon them, and must choose where to devote their resources. This book is devoted more specifically to gun rights in Maine, since Maine is the State of the author's domicile.

With a narrower focus and local grassroots political activism the author has the ability to engage the public in ways which a large, national organization may not.

A comparison: The efforts of the Centers for Disease Control and the National Institutes of Health to promote public health and safety are not able to function in a vacuum. State-level health agencies and local hospitals are necessary to ensure maximal effectiveness of those efforts. Similarly, the NRA may be the largest and most well-known firearm advocacy group in the U.S.A. but they are still but one group.

Carrying A Firearm

2. Why do some people open carry a firearm?

Reasoning differs between individuals. Some of the most frequently cited reasons include:

- Deterrent effect against violent crime;
- To raise visibility of firearms rights issues;
- Comfort, ease of carry, and access to the holster;
- To challenge negative stereotypes about firearms;
- To exercise a constitutional right.

Their objective is to return to full constitutional carry in Maine and other states. This requires the legal and social normalization of firearms in the public mind. This cannot be accomplished without visibility and public interaction.

3. Why do you need a gun?

The right to keep and bear arms is a fundamental natural right which the founders of this country codified into the US Constitution. As such, the exercise of this right should require no justification, just as no one should feel obligated to explain why they want freedom of assembly, religion, or speech.

Moreover, there are many practical reasons to own and carry a firearm. These include, but are not limited to:

- To take responsibility for our own safety - Carrying a weapon responsibly is a declaration of personal autonomy. An individual who carries has decided that his or her personal safety is not to be entrusted to external agents, such as law enforcement or private security.

- To assert their rights - The 2nd Amendment to the US Constitution, and Article 1, Section 16 of the Maine State Constitution protect the right to keep and **bear** arms. A right unexercised is a right potentially lost.

- To be prepared - People wear seatbelts and keep fire extinguishers and smoke detectors in their homes as simple preventative measures to unlikely but possible dangers they may encounter. For many firearm owners the decision to carry a gun is based on the same principles of preparedness. According to the US Bureau of Justice Statistics, Over 1,600,000 Americans were the victim of a serious violent crime (rape, robbery, aggravated assault, and homicide) in 2007, the most recent year for which statistics are available.

It is not the position of this book that everyone should carry a firearm, but it is our position that everyone has the right to do so, and that this should be openly acknowledged to the public. The choice to carry is an involved decision which must not be made lightly.

4. Aren't you just being paranoid?

Paranoia: (n) a psychological disorder characterized by delusions of persecution or grandeur.

The relevant terms are **psychological disorder** and **delusions of persecution**. A gun owner who asserts fairly that he or she is being unjustly denied a constitutional right, or has a reasonable fear that he or she will be, is not paranoid. To be deprived of a right is by definition a form of persecution, and therefore not a delusion.

To address the broader context of whether firearm ownership and carry is inherently "antisocial" or a choice to distance oneself from society and one's peers, the short answer is "no". This perspective reveals more about how society feels about guns than how the gun owner feels about society. Calling a gun owner "paranoid" or "antisocial" is a confusion of terms and in many cases a thinly-veiled ad-hominem attack which attempts to discredit the gun owner by questioning their mental state. Gun owners come from and occupy all walks and stations of life and are broadly representative of the population as a whole.

Legal Issues

5. Is open carry legal in Maine?

Open Carry is legal in Maine without a permit provided that the owner, firearm, and location are not otherwise restricted. Generally speaking, any individual who is otherwise lawfully allowed to own and carry a weapon may open carry that weapon in Maine. All federal laws still apply.

6. Are there exceptions?

Yes. Please see *Maine Gun Carry Laws,* Chapter 20, page 133, for examples of areas and situations where open carry in Maine is not authorized. This list is not intended to be all-inclusive. **Always consult a lawyer in your state first!**

7. Can local municipalities in Maine restrict open carry?

NO. Under Title 25, Part 5, Chapter 252-A of the Maine Revised Statutes state law **pre-empts** all local codes. In other words, no local municipality can enact a legally enforceable restriction on open or concealed firearm carry. That power is reserved for the State of Maine and federal government.

25

Detained For Open Carry

TRANSCRIPT: — 18 AUG 2010 — *"Detained by Biddeford Maine Police Department for Open Carry."*

Detainee: *Can I ask you why you are stopping me?*
Officer: *You have a gun on you.*
Detainee: *Is that illegal in Maine?*
Officer: *What's that?*
Detainee: *Is that illegal in Maine?*
Officer: *Where are you from?*
Detainee: *Am I free to go?*
Officer: *Nope. Not at this point in time.*
Detainee: *What crime are you investigating me for?*
Officer: *You're carrying a gun on you. And I would like to know what for . . .*
Detainee: *Is that illegal in Maine?*
Officer: *Do you have any ID on you?*
Detainee: *Am I doing anything that requires an ID?*
Officer: *Do you have an ID on you?*
Detainee: *Yes, I do.*
Officer: *Can I see it?*
Detainee: *Um . . . No . . . unless you're writing a summons or arresting me . . . Um . . . then I'd be required to show you my ID, but if I'm not doing anything that requires an ID I'd rather just be on my way.*
Officer: *Do you refuse to be identified?*
Detainee: *Um . . . am I doing anything illegal?*
Officer: *What's that?*

Detainee: *Am I doing anything illegal?*

Officer: *I need to figure that out. I need to get you to identify yourself in order to figure that out.*

Detainee: *You can't detain me unless you believe that I'm committing or about to commit a crime.*

Officer: *OK. If you have bail conditions that say you can't have weapons on you, you will be committing a crime. So I have to get you identified.*

Detainee: *Do you believe I have bail conditions that would say . . .*

Officer: *I don't know, so that's why I have to get you identified.*

Detainee: *If you don't know, then you have no reasons to stop me . . . Can you get a supervisor here so that we can get it straightened out?*

Female Officer: *I got a complaint, actually, in the parking lot they saw a male walking around with a gun on his hip.*

Detainee: *Is that illegal?*

Female Officer: *We're not saying that's illegal but we need to know who you are and identify you.*

Detainee: *Am I free to go then?*

Female Officer: *We need to know who you are because we need to know if you have a legal weapons permit [inaudible] because that's the only way we can know, by asking you your name. We don't know you just like you don't know our name.*

Detainee: *I would like to not be questioned without the presence of an attorney and I invoke my right to remain silent then.*

Female Officer: *We're not here to try to give you a hard time. [Inaudibly] my concern for just asking your* name. *Are you on bail conditions?*

Detainee: *No.*

Female Officer: *Have you ever been in trouble?*

Detainee: *Um . . . I was arrested once but the charges were dropped.*

Female Officer: *Then that shouldn't be a problem . . . we just have to verify . . . do you have . . .*

Detainee: *I would like the presence of an attorney if you're going to continue to question me. Then I would like to invoke my right to remain silent.*

Male Officer: *OK . . . it would make it a whole lot easier if you'd just let us see your ID, Sir.*

Detainee: *Am I required to show you my ID by law? . . . You're detaining me illegally if you don't believe that I've committed a crime . . . then you're detaining me illegally right now and I would like to . . .*

Officer: *[Inaudible] whether or not you are committing a crime we have to determine who you are.*

Detainee: *If you don't have any reasonable suspicion that I have committed a crime, then you can't detain me.*

Female Officer: *You have a gun on you.*

Detainee: *Um . . .*

Female Officer: *It's highly unusual activity . . .*

Detainee: *Have you ever seen someone openly carrying who is committing a crime . . . ever?*

Female Officer: *[Inaudible]*

Detainee: *What is your reasonable suspicion?*

Female Officer: *[inaudible] what your intentions are . . . Our duty as police officers [inaudible] to find out who it is and being aware of what's going on in our environment.*

Detainee: *In a legal manner.*

Female Officer: *[Inaudible] that's what we're doing.*

Detainee: *You have no reason to detain me right now. You have no reasonable suspicion that I've committed a crime.*

Female Officer: *Yes . . .*

Detainee: *So I'd like to be on my way.*

Female Officer: *We have a complaint [inaudible] . . .*

Detainee: *Unless you have reasonable suspicion that it is legitimate then you can't detain me for it.*

Half minute of silence.

Male Officer: *[Inaudible]*

Detainee: *You're Rosso . . . Russo . . . and Cala . . . ?*

Quarter minute of silence.

Officer: *[Inaudible]*

Detainee: *Um . . . it's copies of some laws in Maine . . . Copies of the Constitution.*

Officer: *Are from this state?*

Detainee: *Yes I am. . . Um . . . I don't know why you continue to ask me some questions after I asked for an attorney . . . but . . . Um . . . I'm . . .*

One-half minute of silence.

Again, what crime am I being detained for . . . What are you detaining me for?

Female Officer: *[Inaudible] get calls for either suspicious activity, suspicious [inaudible], suspicious people. We have to identify who the person is.*

Detainee: *You have to have a suspicion of crime that you're detaining me for . . . Is there a suspicion of crime right now?*

Female Officer: *We have citizens that are concerned . . .*

Detainee: *That doesn't matter, unfortunately . . . Um . . . You can't detain someone without a suspicion of crime. So even if someone is sitting in a car . . . Is that a crime? If there's no crime . . . as soon as you determine that there is no crime, you should let me go . . . And . . .*

Female Officer: *We need to determine that in order to figure our who you are . . .*

Detainee: *You have no reason to believe that I have committed a crime, do you?*

Female Officer: *We need to know who you are.*

Detainee: *What crime are you detaining me for?*

Female Officer: *[inaudible] suspicious activity.*

Detainee: *What crime are you detaining me for?*

Female Officer: *[inaudible] suspicious activity.*

Detainee: *OK, then what statute is suspicious activity?*

Female Officer: *We're investigating . . .*

Detainee: *What statute is suspicious activity, I'd just like to be on my way.*

Female Officer: *We got a complaint and we are investigating it . . .*

Detainee: *Why do you need to identify me?*

Female Officer: *To see if you have any bail conditions.*

Detainee: *Do you have any reasonable belief that I am?*

Female Officer: *[Inaudible]*

Detainee: *OK.*

Male Officer: *We have to put your name and information on report and* [inaudible] *I'd like to get that* [inaudible] . . .

Detainee: *Um . . . do you have any reason to take my name?*

Officer: *We need to be able to* [inaudible] *dispatch* [inaudible] *a report of a man walking around with a firearm, in case they get calls again, which they probably will . . . because it's causing the people* [inaudible] *we need to know who you are.*

Detainee: *Am I required by law to give you my name?*
Officer: *What?*

Detainee: *Am I required by law to give you my name?*
Officer: *I need it for my report.*

Detainee: *You can write whatever you want in your report. . . but I don't have to give you my name.*

Three long minutes of silence.

Detainee: *Am I free to go now?*
Officer: *After I get your name.*

Detainee: *Ok . . . Um . . . I would rather not . . . I'm not required to by law . . . and I'd just rather be on my way . . . and I don't understand why I'm being held up.*

One-half minute of silence.

Officer: [Inaudible] *to make my report.*
Detainee: *Um . . . Am I free to go?*

One minute of silence.

Officer: *I need your address and phone number.*

Detainee: *If I'm not required by law to give that to you, then I would just rather be on my way . . . if your looking for the law that requires me to provide you with my name . . . it's 17a and 15a . . .*

Officer: *[Inaudible]*

Detainee: *I have a copy of that law in my pocket if you want to see it. It says I don't have to . . . well I have to if you're issuing me a summons . . . but If your not issuing me a summons I don't have to identify myself to you . . . and I don't see why I'm being held.*

One minute of silence.

Detainee: *Am I free to go yet?*

One minute more of silence.

Detainee: *Am I still being detained or am I free to go?*

One-half minute of silence. (Ed., silence equals consent).

Detainee: *I'm going to assume that I'm free to go, then . . . I mean, am I free to go? . . . I'm going to assume that I'm free to go . . . and I'm going to take off. Have a good day.*

Norman and Shane

Shane Belanger Founded
The Maine Open Carry Association
http://maineopencarry.org

To View **"Detained For Open Carry"** On YouTube:
http://tinyurl.com/3jbpyzp

Author's Comment

It took a great deal of alertness, courage and awareness for this young man to stand up for his rights in the knowledgeable way that he did.

We live in a civilized society. He had every right to do what he did. This isn't about legal carry. This is about the police and their treatment of the population that they serve.

No animosity was shown by either party. Both parties were somewhat stressed but handled this situation very well.

Whether the officers or the detainee knew it or not, had he not answered each question with a question — had he instead complied with the officer's commands — he would have voluntarily, though unknowingly, placed himself within the jurisdiction of the state and he would have been open to possible arrest, regardless of the law, although the charge would have more than likely been dismissed.

The young man gave them no indication that he **"understood"** — i.e., no indication that he "stood under" — what they were trying to do which was to **get him to voluntarily assess himself in the matter;** putting him totally under their control.

Had he complied with their requests, he would have forfeited his right to be treated: as **"innocent until proven guilty"** — instead of **"guilty until proven innocent"** — which he was not.

After Altercation, Philadelphia Police Say They Won't Look the Other Way on Open-Carry Gun Owners

By Stephen Clark , May 21, 2011.

Mark Fiorino, a suburban Philadelphia IT worker, is in legal trouble after posting to YouTube an audiotape of his encounter with Philadelphia police over his unconcealed handgun.

With a shocking altercation between Philadelphia police and a 25-year-old IT worker putting the spotlight back on open-carry gun laws, local authorities are warning gun owners that they will be "inconvenienced" if they carry unconcealed handguns in the city.

Lt. Raymond Evers, a spokesman for the city police, told FoxNews.com that gun owners who open carry, **which is legal in the city,** may be asked to lay on the ground until officers feel safe while they check permits.

"Philadelphia, in certain areas, is very dangerous," he said. "There's a lot of gun violence." Several officers have been killed in the line of duty in the past three years, local authorities say.

The warning comes after Mark Fiorino, a suburban Philadelphia IT worker, posted a 15 minute audiotape to YouTube of his tense, 45-minute encounter with police in February over his exposed handgun. The video went viral and captured national attention.

After Fiorino released the audiotape, he was charged with disorderly conduct and reckless endangerment. He now faces up to two years in prison.

The police department and assistant district attorney are coming after me, in my opinion, to make an example of me because I stood up to them and exposed them for their lack of knowledge," Fiorino said, who called the trial "absolutely inappropriate and a waste of taxpayer money."

Fiorino said he did nothing reckless, nor did he endanger anyone's life.

"I had a gun pointed at my chest," he said.

Only seven states ban the practice of openly carrying guns, and Pennsylvania isn't one of them, according to OpenCarry.org, which advocates gun rights.

In Philadelphia, a permit is required to carry handguns openly. But on Feb. 13 a police sergeant who was unaware of the law — which dates back to at least 1996 when the state Supreme Court referenced it in an unrelated ruling — stopped Fiorino, who was walking to an auto parts shop in Northeast Philadelphia with a gun on his hip.

Sgt. Michael Dougherty can be heard yelling out to Fiorino as "Junior," and asking him to show his hands as Fiorino protests having a gun pointed at his chest, prompting

Dougherty to call for backup. Dougherty grows increasingly agitated as Fiorino offers to show his permit when he is ordered to get on his knees, causing Dougherty to threaten to shoot if he makes a move. Dougherty then unleashed a string of profanities as the two argued over the legality of open carry.

"Do you know you can't openly carry here in Philadelphia?" Dougherty yells.

"Yes, you can, if you have a license to carry firearms," Fiorino responds. "It's Directive 137. It's your own internal directive."

When several other officers arrive, Fiorino is forced to the ground as he tries to explain that he's not breaking the law."

Shut the f—— up!" Dougherty yells.

Police found the recorder while searching Fiorino's pockets. Officers eventually released him after speaking to the department's lawyer and being told that he was within his legal rights.

Police Commissioner Charles Ramsey took issue with Dougherty's language and his lack of knowledge about the law during the altercation, Evers said, but not with the stop itself.

Evers, who has been an officer for nearly 20 years, said "very rarely do people open carry in Philadelphia." But he added he wasn't make excuses."

"We weren't as up on that crime code as we should have been," he said, adding that officers are being re-educated on open carry in response to the incident.

Dougherty is facing disciplinary action pending the outcome of an internal affairs investigation, Evers said.

Fiorino's trial is scheduled to begin in July and the district attorney's office emphasizes that Fiorino's response to the police, not his gun rights, are at issue."

This office respects and upholds the rights of a citizen to lawfully carry a firearm," Tasha Jamerson, a spokeswoman for the district attorney's office, said in a statement emailed to FoxNews.com. "

The permit to carry a concealed weapon, however, does not mean that a permit-holder can abuse that right by refusing to cooperate with police."

Jamerson said Fiorino "allegedly became belligerent and hostile" when police officers "were legally attempting to investigate a potential crime."

But Fiorino's attorney, Joseph Valvo, said the case is larger than Fiorino."

It's my position that this entire prosecution is an effort by Philadelphia authorities to send a message to legitimate gun owners that open carry as a practice is not welcome in Philadelphia **despite the fact that it's constitutionally protected behavior** and that's offensive to me as a citizen and as a lawyer," Valvo said.

Gun rights advocates say they're are also offended.

John Pierce, a co-founder of OpenCarry.org said, Philadelphia police have sent a clear message to gun owners that will chill their rights to openly carry."

"Even if it's legal, we can punish you financially and by disruptions in your life," he said.

But the district attorney's office dismissed as "ludicrous" claims it is seeking retaliation or "trying to send a message."

This office only charges people with offenses that we think we can prosecute," Tasha Jamerson said in an interview with FoxNews.com. "

We just don't willy-nilly charge a person with a crime as

retaliation for an incident."

The February incident wasn't the first time Philadelphia police officers have confronted Fiorino about his unconcealed gun. Since July, he has been stopped twice and he has had an audio recorder on him each time "in case a cop is having a bad day or doesn't understand the law", he said.

His handgun was confiscated once for five months, but neither occasion escalated like the third encounter.

Fiorino said he studied Pennsylvania law for a year before he started openly carrying a gun. He said he carries the gun openly because some of his friends have been held up at gunpoint and he's not willing to allow himself to be helpless.

Police spokesman Evers said Fiorino appears to be inviting trouble from the law by "surreptitiously" recording his encounters with police."

If you put everything together, it was more than him walking down the street to go to an auto parts store — without a jacket in the middle of winter," Evers said.

But Fiorino denies that he was looking for trouble."

How many times does a convenience store need to be robbed to be justified in putting up a security system?" he said.

To Hear **"Fiorino's 15 minute audio of the 45 minute violation of his Rights for Open Carry"** On YouTube:
http://tinyurl.com/4oyok6d

Gun Carry In the USA

Gun Maintenance & Care

Gun Owners' Storage Guidelines

Each year we hear about children and adults who are injured or killed in gun related accidents. In 2002 alone, 254 children between the ages of 1 and 14 died in homicides involving firearms. 86 children in the same age group committed suicide using a firearm and 59 died as a result of firearm related accidents. Many if not all of these deaths could have been prevented by simply making sure firearms were secured safely.

It is the responsibility of the firearms owner to know how to safely handle and secure their firearms.

Most states impose some form of legal duty on adults to take reasonable steps to deny access by children to dangerous substances or instruments. It is the individual gun owner's responsibility to understand and follow all laws regarding gun purchase, ownership, storage, and transport.

If you choose to own a gun, you have a responsibility to set a positive example.

As a firearm owner, you must make absolutely sure that guns in your home are stored so that they are not accessible to children or other unauthorized persons. Hiding a gun in a closet, drawer or similar location is not safe storage. Children are extremely curious and might find a gun in your home that you thought was safely hidden or inaccessible. As with most all areas of home safety, your objective as a firearm owner is to put in place a series of simple precautions or multiple safeguards that together help create a secure environment for firearms in the home.

Each of these precautions is designed to provide an additional barrier against unauthorized use.

Storing Firearms in a Safe Manner-

• Store guns and ammunition so they are not accessible to unauthorized persons.

• Unloaded firearms should be stored in a locked cabinet, safe, gun vault or storage case. Be sure to place a locked storage case in a location inaccessible to children.

• Unloaded firearms can also be secured with a gun locking device that renders the firearm inoperable.

• Store ammunition in a locked location separate from firearms.

• Remember, nearly all firearms accidents in the home can be prevented simply by making sure that guns are kept unloaded and locked up, with ammunition secured in a separate location.

Firearms Safety Rules For Kids-

1. Don't Touch!
2. Leave the Area!
3. Tell an Adult!

If you find a gun, don't pick it up! Just leave it alone! And tell an adult right away.

Cable Lock

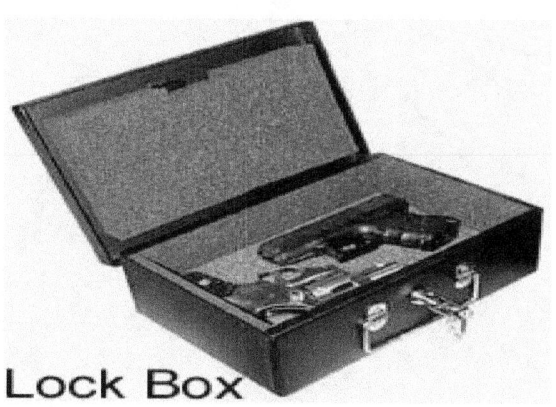

Lock Box

Pistol Correction Chart
(Right Hand)

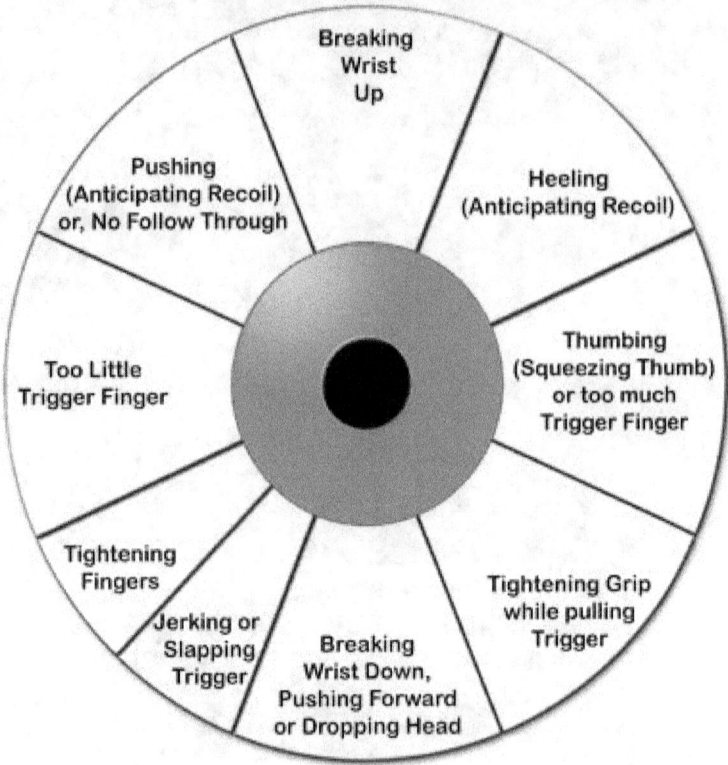

- Breaking Wrist Up
- Pushing (Anticipating Recoil) or, No Follow Through
- Heeling (Anticipating Recoil)
- Too Little Trigger Finger
- Thumbing (Squeezing Thumb) or too much Trigger Finger
- Tightening Fingers
- Jerking or Slapping Trigger
- Breaking Wrist Down, Pushing Forward or Dropping Head
- Tightening Grip while pulling Trigger

Basic Gun Safety Rules

1. <u>Always</u> keep the firearm pointed in a safe direction.

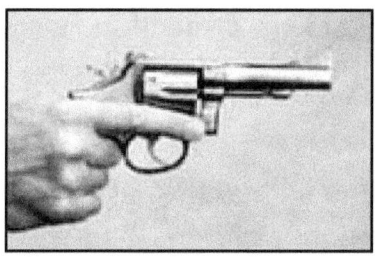

2. <u>Always</u> keep your finger off the trigger until ready to shoot.

3. <u>Always</u> keep the gun unloaded until ready to use.

Additional Rules For Gun Safety

4. <u>Know</u> your target and what is beyond.

5. <u>Know</u> how to use your gun safely.

6. <u>Be sure</u> your gun is safe to operate.

7. <u>Use only</u> the correct ammunition for your gun.

8. <u>Wear</u> eye and ear protection as appropriate.

9. <u>Never</u> use alcohol or drugs before or while shooting.

10. <u>Store</u> guns so that they are inaccessible to unauthorized persons.

11. <u>Be aware</u> that certain types of guns and many shooting activities require additional safety precautions.

Your Right to Self-defense 165

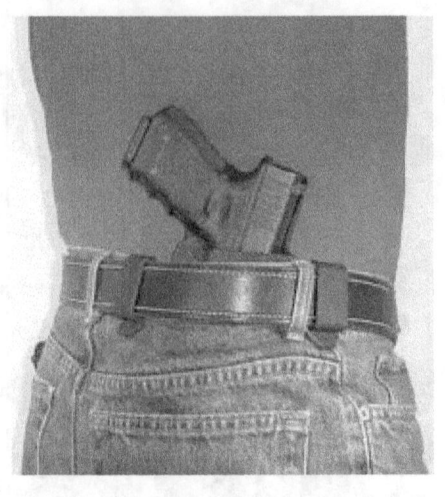

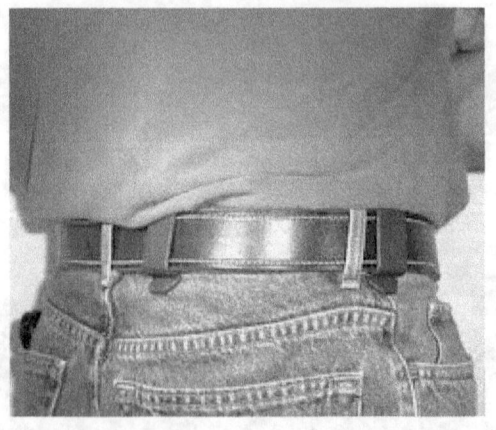

Words To The Wise

For many, the term *personal protection* immediately evokes images of martial-arts techniques or a handgun in a nightstand. In truth, however, the use of force, or deadly force, is only one of many methods that you can employ to defend life and limb, and indeed is used only as a last resort when other methods have failed.

For many ethical, legal and practical reasons, it is always preferable to escape, evade, deter, or otherwise avoid an attack, rather than be forced to counter an attack with force.

Even when planning and skill give you an overwhelming advantage over an assailant, sidestepping a violent confrontation is always the best course.

There may be times, however, when circumstances allow no other option but the use of force to save your life, or the lives of your family or friends. Under such circumstances, a firearm — most commonly, a handgun — is unquestionably the most effective defensive tool available; if it is used properly.

Special Reports

　　　Gun Carry In the USA

Senate Seeks To Create Caesar

May 16, 2011, by Terresa Monroe-Hamilton

While all of America is distracted and focused on the death of Osama bin Laden, our President and his minions have been fast at work laying the groundwork for S. 679: Presidential Appointment Efficiency and Streamlining Act of 2011, to speed through the Senate and make its way into the House and then to the President to sign. Yes, the other hand is quickly forming into a dictatorial fist that is about to smash our Constitution.

As you will recall, the beginning of the end of liberty in Rome commenced with Augustus Caesar who compromised the authority of the Senate through the force of arms and basically the Senate became a facade. America is poised, with this proposed bill, to morph immediately from a Democratic Republic into an empire with the privileged eunuchs of the Senate as window dressing, and a dictator – the first American Caesar – at the country's helm.

And leading the progressive charge is Chuck Schumer (D-NY). No big surprise there. Schumer is an elitist Marxist and a first class progressive who hates America almost as much as he loves power. He introduced S. 679 on March 30th, 2011. He was joined by a gaggle of progressives from the left and the right. This is something we have been warning Americans about for a long time. If we are to survive as a nation, we must rid ourselves of ALL progressives, or our nation is doomed, and freedom will be swept into the dustbin of history. Schumer's esteemed list of constitutional traitors is as follows:

* Sen. Lamar Alexander (R-TN)
* Sen. Jeff Bingaman (D-NM)
* Sen. Richard Blumenthal (D-CT)
* Sen. Scott Brown (R-MA)
* Sen. Thomas Carper (D-DE)
* Sen. Susan Collins (R-ME)
* Sen. Richard Durbin (D-IL)
* Sen. Mike Johanns (R-NE)
* Sen. Jon Kyl (R-AZ)
* Sen. Joseph Lieberman (I-CT)
* Sen. Richard Lugar (R-IN)
* Sen. Mitch McConnell (R-KY)
* Sen. John Reed (D-RI)
* Sen. Harry Reid (D-NV)
* Sen. Sheldon Whitehouse (D-RI)

From The Heritage Foundation, here is a succinct explanation of the bill:

"The bill reduces the number of presidential appointments that require the consent of the Senate and establishes within the executive branch a Working Group on Streamlining Paperwork for Executive Nominations. Individuals nominated to senior executive offices suffer slow and detailed background investigations and mounds of duplicative paperwork before a President sends their nominations to the Senate. After nomination, many nominees suffer time-consuming inaction or time-consuming and excruciating action as the Senate proceeds (or does not) with consideration of the nomination. The sponsors of S. 679 have identified a valid problem, but proposed the wrong solution. Congress should not enact S. 679."

In essence they want to give the President the sole power to appoint people to positions of his choosing within our government.

Obama would be free to do this without the approval of the Senate. Senate approval of such positions is mandated by the U.S. Constitution in Article II, Section 2 under the "Appointments Clause":

"... he shall nominate, and by and with the Advice and Consent of the Senate, shall appoint Ambassadors, other public Ministers and Consuls, Judges of the supreme Court, and all other Officers of the United States, whose Appointments are not herein otherwise provided for, and which shall be established by Law: but the Congress may by Law vest the Appointment of such inferior Officers, as they think proper, in the President alone, in the Courts of Law, or in the Heads of Departments." (Emphasis added).

This bill will do away with the checks and balances that separate an American Form of government from those such as Venezuela and Brazil.

Already we have power mongers such as Cass Sunstein, our Regulatory Czar (more commonly known as the Office of Information and Regulatory Affairs and more aptly titled the Office of Government Propaganda), running amok across the US using agencies such as the EPA as a weapon of regulation and control. There is not a single area in our country that Sunstein does not have his hands into. This should scare Americans, but all I hear are crickets. The silence of capitulation seals our fate as surely as the thunderous applause of approval – so ends the Republic.

More from The Heritage Foundation:

"When the delegates of the states gathered in Philadelphia in the summer of 1787 and wrote the Constitution, they distributed the powers of the federal government among two Houses of Congress, a President, and a judiciary, and required in many cases that two of them work together to exercise a particular constitutional power. That separation of powers protects the liberties of the American people by preventing any one officer of the government from aggregating too much power.

"The Framers of the Constitution did not give the President the kingly power to appoint the senior officers of the government by himself. Instead, they allowed the President to name an individual for a senior office, but then required the President to obtain the Senate's consent before appointing the individual to office. Thus, they required the cooperation of the President and the Senate to put someone in high office."

Americans have not forgotten about Obama's string of Czars. Czars that he was supposed to downsize or get rid of. Czars, which in our personal viewpoint, were and still are illegal under the Constitution. But progressives never go away, they just shift... as has done so many of Obama's Czars.

With this sweeping bill, more than 200 positions will no longer require Senate approval. Obama will dictate who his powerful lieutenants are and who will control America. The Senate will merely be a sham to parrot Obama's dictates. With this bill, checks and balances will be effectively nullified. What does that portend you say?

One day, your right to own a gun will be gone, just regulated away. Businesses will be nationalized even more than they are now. Heavy regulation will ensue concerning communications and the Internet. Many private businesses will wither and die. You will be told what and how much to eat – food and gas rationing will become the norm. Poverty and squalor will become equal for all as wealth is redistributed to other nations.

If there are elections, they will be a joke and pointless. There will be a few powerful elites and then the masses. Guess which camp you and I will be in?

Our best hope at this juncture is that this abomination will be stopped in the House. We must weed out the progressives and we must win in 2012. This country will not survive another four years of progressive policies; not as a Democratic Republic and not as a free entity anyway.

The bitter irony on display here, is that the same jackals that have barked and snarled and feigned horror at "American Imperialism," are the very ones who now howl their support for a true American Empire. All hail Caesar!

Since taking office in January 2009. Obama has been busy appointing "czars" to further balloon his administration into the largest in the history of the presidency. Some of these appointed positions include:

• The much needed "Asian Carp Czar", John Goss, who was appointed in September 2010 to simply be the federal watchdog over a fish! Find that in the Constitution!

• What about the "Global Warming Czar", Carol Browner? Her sole job is to continue pushing the fallacy of global warming to Americans and the liberal lunacy propagated by President Obama that we need to buy more tiny cars more akin to lawnmowers than automobiles so that we can plug them in for a whole 40 mile roundtrip spin. Even worse is her ideology! Ms. Browner, again appointed by President Obama, was a leader in the Socialist Commission for a Sustainable World Society.

• Of course you also have the "Ethics Czar" or "Transparency Czar", a joke in and of itself in regards to a man in Obama who promised the most transparent presidency in history only to be the most secretive and manipulative Administration in our nation's history. His name - Norm Eisen, an old law school friend of Obama that was never confirmed for the post, as he was accused of firing an Inspector General for partisan political purposes. Later, Obama simply elevated Mr. Eisen to the position through an unconstitutional recess appointment.

• We also have a "Science Czar", John Holdren. This man authored a book advocating forced abortions and mass sterilization. Folks, that is scary, and dare we say, Hitleresque? Yet, he apparently fits right in at 1600 Pennsylvania Avenue.

• Who can forget another Obama Czar, Cass Sunstein, and the "Regulatory Czar". Obama's "Regulatory Czar" isn't a fan of the First Amendment ... you know, the one that guarantees free speech. Instead, Mr. Sunstein, again the man Obama tapped as his regulation go-to-guy, was quoted as saying "in light of astonishing economic and technological changes, we must doubt whether, as interpreted, the constitutional guarantee of free speech is adequately serving democratic goals." Sunstein also once wrote that he believe animals should have the right to sue humans for neglect! Again, he's Obama's regulatory man.

• Then, finally, there is the all-important "Green Jobs Czar", Mr. Van Jones. Van Jones served as the "Green Jobs Czar" only from March to September 2009, after his past of Marxist leanings and 9/11 conspiratorial theories were brought to light.

What "Great Americans" Obama has illegally appointed to self-created positions! These people have absolutely NOTHING in common with the heart of America! Do you have neighbors clamoring for mass sterilization and forced abortions? Do you have friends who believe Fluffy the cat should be able to sue her owners, or whose neighbors were leaders of Socialist groups at one time?

America is in trouble. We are on cusp of the impossible happening in America because we have a Congress that has surrendered its power to legislate to a White House determined to rule by decree. We are watching the Congress of Sleepy Hollow sleep instead of taking the action needed right now to stop this assault on our nation from its own presidency.

It is estimated that Obama now has 32 of these "Czars", all of which are unnecessary, cost taxpayers millions of dollars, and which are not mentioned anywhere in the Constitution. It is alarming that the Chief Executive of the United States is creating fictitious jobs that are in no way authorized by our U.S. Constitution - and, in fact, are created in order to bypass that sacred document!

The individuals Obama has appointed don't stand for American ideals; they are Leftists of the highest order.

President Obama has shown a blatant disregard for the law time and time again during less than three years in office. Consider these:

•   He pushed through OBAMACARE, despite it being illegal for the government to require you to purchase a service;

•   He denied thousands of military personnel and their families the right to vote during this past election by FAILING to enforce the MOVE Act! He is the leader of the Executive Branch and he failed to enforce the law in regards to voting, perhaps the most precious right we have as Americans.

•   He dropped the lawsuit against the RACIST BLACK PANTHERS, even though they committed a felony by intimidating voters during the 2008 Election!

He repeatedly bypasses Congress as he gains control:

Climate Control - The EPA is punishing states and industry through carbon and greenhouse gas regulations ... because Obama couldn't get climate legislation through Congress. Let's be perfectly clear: The United States Constitution and the United States Congress does NOT give the EPA the authority to regulate anything!

Union Control - Obama is pushing Card Check legislation, which would take away secret ballots from workers and influence union elections. His Labor Department is also threatening to sue states who don't comply! Obama desperately needs the money from union coffers to win reelection and he will do anything to make sure that the money, taken straight from the wages of working Americans, is available come time for reelection.

Land Control - The Department of the Interior created a new designation, "Wild Lands," through Secretarial Order, giving the government control of millions of acres of land ... because Congress didn't pass America's Great Outdoors Act.

Internet Control - Four days before Christmas, the Liberal FCC took over Internet content ... even though three judges in three separate cases warned they had no right to do so!

Gun Control - The BATF is attempting backdoor gun control by requiring people who buy "too many" weapons to register them ... because Congress cannot pass gun registration laws. The ATF does NOT have the Constitutional or Congressional power to register guns.

Open Borders Control - Obama instructed ICE to ignore the Constitution's laws on illegal aliens, and he hauled Arizona before the U.N. Human Rights Council to protest their immigration laws ... because Congress didn't pass the illegal immigration bills he wanted.

So, what will you do? Will you, like so many others, simply look the other way while the America we hold dear wastes away as the Dictator-in-Chief, Barack Obama, continues his socialist ways?

The Right to keep and bear Arms

By Rico S. Giron, Future Sheriff of San Miguel County, General election, Nov. 2, 2010.

The Right to keep and bear arms shall NOT be infringed.

The united States of America was born at the point of a gun. Our American Heritage is that every American is born with a gun in their Right Hand, the Holy Book in their Left Hand and Revolution and Defiance in their Hearts. We the People of this great country have always defied injustice, oppression and tyranny. Now we are faced with injustice, oppression and tyranny from our own Federal "government". The Federal "government" is Public Enemy # 1.

Go to www.sheriffmack.com

The Second Amendment is America's Last Freedom. The Second Amendment puts teeth into this Constitution for the united States of America. The Right of Self Defense is a God-given Right that no man, corporation or government can remove or abrogate. This God-given Right was recognized by the Founding Fathers of this country and thus wanting to make sure that all future governments clearly understood it, they put it to writing.

We are born with the Bill of Rights as our Birthright gifted to us by Almighty God. No man can remove what God has given us. No man can rend asunder that which our Lord and Creator has given to us.

The words "shall not be infringed" are loud and clear for all to understand. The law says what it means and means what it says. Only anti-gun factions misinterpret these clearly written words.

The Bill of Rights is a warning to all governments that these Rights are God-given and cannot, and will not, be removed from the hands and Hearts of the People of America.

Here in the Republic of New Mexico, the State Constitution recognizes these Inherent Rights. Section 4 of the New Mexico Constitution clearly states:

"All persons are born equally free, and have certain natural, inherent and inalienable rights, among which are the rights of enjoying and defending life and liberty, of acquiring, possessing and protecting property, and of seeking and obtaining safety and happiness".

Defending life and liberty:

Clearly then, without being able to defend our life and liberty, having them does not mean anything. Without being able to defend our life and liberty, then the words of section 4 above would amount to nothing more than lip service with no substance.

Acquiring, possessing and protecting property: To acquire and possess without the ability to defend and protect property would also amount to nothing more than empty words.

The Founding Fathers did not write the Bill of Rights to have them be empty words. No sir! They wrote them as a warning to the future governments that they knew would one day attempt to remove these God given rights. We as American Citizens must understand that the Bill of Rights cannot be modified, abrogated or removed by any government, any corporation or any man.

In Article II, section 6, of the Constitution for the Republic of New Mexico it is clearly stated: "No law shall abridge the right of the Citizen to keep and bear arms for security and defense…" **The word, "bear" means to carry. So no state law can tell any Citizen how to carry his/her gun.**

This clearly ties into section 4 above. We have the natural, inherent and inalienable right of "seeking and obtaining safety and happiness". We as Citizens decide for ourselves how to obtain these. If We the Citizens decide that carrying a concealed gun will best accomplish our own safety and happiness, then the STATE OF NEW MEXICO, cannot under any circumstances tell We the Citizens that We cannot carry a concealed gun.

However, there exists a contradiction in section 6, it also states: **"but nothing herein shall be held to permit the carrying of concealed weapons. No municipality or county shall regulate, in any way, an incident of the right to keep and bear arms."**

This statement is self-contradicting. If no municipality or county can regulate the right to keep and bear arms, then they cannot tell any Citizens the "how" and "when" of keeping and bearing arms. So the prohibition of "carrying of concealed weapons" is self-contradictory and in violation of the Supremacy of this Constitution for the united States of America. **Again, anything that is out of harmony with the Supremacy of the Constitution for the united States of America, is null and void, self-canceling, and non-existent.**

For this very reason I will not book into the County Jail any law abiding Citizen charged with carrying a concealed gun. Every Sovereign, law abiding Citizen must decide how and when to arm themselves. That is not the business of the servant state police or city police. The Right to Bear Arms is between each Citizen and God.

In addition, my Office of Sheriff will conduct classes on self defense, carrying of a concealed weapon, Constitutional Law, the Citizens' arrest powers of all Citizens in the county.

We the People have the right of self-defense against all oppressors, criminals and attackers, including any government — whether this government be Federal, State, County or City — that is dedicated to oppressing the God-given Right to Keep and Bear Arms.

Historically, tyrants have always prepared the Citizens of their country for dis-arming by passing oppressive laws that criminalize the owning of guns and rifles for self-defense. Here in this country, there are approximately 20,000 gun control laws already in existence. Each and every one of these so-called "laws" are unlawful and un-Constitutional and thus, null and void, and self-canceling.

This Constitution for the united States of America is the Supreme Law of the Land. Any statute or law out of harmony with this Constitution is null and void from the beginning. Any court decision that is out of harmony with this Constitution, is null and void.

The Bill of Rights clarified for the government, that the rights enumerated therein, are God-given rights, not rights given to men by other men or governments, and that these rights are Sacred and untouchable. They cannot be removed or abrogated by any government or any man or any corporation, under any circumstance. In the simplest terms possible this means that the Second Amendment prohibits any and all gun control.

So then, we come to the glaring contradiction: If all 20,000 of these gun control laws are in fact out of harmony with the Supremacy of the Constitution for the united States of America via the Second Amendment, then all 20,000 gun control laws are null and void, self-canceling, and actually non-existent. They are no more than illusions of control through ignorance and FEAR.

Every American must stand up and say to the anti-gun advocates, "You can take my gun from my cold, dead fingers." [read Sheriff Richard Mack's book, "From my Cold Dead Fingers"]. For that very reason, I will never confiscate any weapons from any law-abiding Citizens of San Miguel County at any time or under any circumstances.

While I am Sheriff of San Miguel County, if any order comes down from the "Executive office" — the '"PRESIDENT OF THE UNITED STATES" — to disarm the Citizens of San Miguel County, I will wholeheartedly disobey that order and tell people to arm themselves and buy more guns and more ammo.

— Rico S. Giron, Future Sheriff of San Miguel County, General election, Nov. 2, 2010.

Sheriff's Volunteer Posse
[*Homeland* Homeland Security]

By Rico S. Giron, Future Sheriff of San Miguel County, General election, Nov. 2, 2010.

I will re-instate the Sheriff's Volunteer Posse to assist the Sheriff's Department.

I will look to have 1,000 Posse Members.

Every able-bodied man and woman will be eligible to be a member of Sheriff's Volunteer Posse, and will be required to be armed at all times to assist in keeping the peace and law enforcement duties.

All members of the Sheriff's Volunteer Posse will be deputized to allow them to protect their families, their properties and their neighbor's life and property.

Warning to all Citizens! This Sheriff's Volunteer Posse will not be a vigilante group bent on pistol-whipping people into submission or people seeking revenge on someone.

Before any volunteer becomes a member of the Sheriff's Volunteer Posse, each member must attend eight hours of training in the Sheriff's Volunteer Posse Mini-Academy.

On a weekly cycle basis, my deputies and I will conduct weekly two hour classes wherein the topics taught will include, but not be limited to: Constitutional Law, specifically the Bill of Rights; Statutory Law; the Common Law Doctrine of Citizen's Arrest, including the issuing of Arrest Warrants by Citizens; and the study of Appeals Court cases and Supreme Court cases dealing with Citizen's Arrest.

Further classes will be developed and added as needed. Volunteer and professional presenters will be actively sought to teach the Mini-Academy, and assist in teaching other classes as needed.

Each volunteer will make a personal commitment to uphold the Law of the Land; respect, and protect Citizen's Rights, and assist the Sheriff's Department in making arrests when necessary. Men and women of exceptional moral character will be recruited. Each and every volunteer will take the same Oath of Office that I as Sheriff of San Miguel County take.

There will be no room for personal vendettas, teaching of lessons or revenges, by Posse members. Each and every Posse member will be held accountable for his/her own actions as Citizens of San Miguel County. If any Posse member disavows his Oath of Office and violates the Rights of any Citizen of San Miguel County, the Posse member will face charges the same as any Citizen committing a crime.

Members of the Sheriff's Volunteer Posse will have the opportunity to interface with members of the New Mexico Sheriff's Association and with members of the National Sheriff's Association by attending the state-wide and nation-wide conferences.

My plan is to have 1,000 members in the Sheriff''s Volunteer Posse with full arrest powers, across the entire county. I plan to deputize the Volunteer Fire Departments in the county. My office will offer concealed carry classes to Citizens and my office will deputize all new licensees

— Rico S. Giron, Future Sheriff of San Miguel County, General election, Nov. 2, 2010.

"Government is a dangerous servant and a fearful master." — George Washington

Gun Carry In the USA

"When the people fear their government, there is tyranny, when the government fears the people, there is liberty." — Thomas Jefferson

"The right of the people to bear arms is not dependent upon the Constitution for its existence." — United States v. Cruikshank

US Supreme Court, 1876.

"A well-regulated Militia, being necessary to the security of a free State, the right of the people to keep and bear Arms, shall not be infringed." — The 2nd Article of the Bill of Rights

Gun Carry In the USA

"No rights are respected but those that are maintained by force." — Chief Justice John Marshall

OTHER PUBLICATIONS

NESARA: National *Economic Security and Reformation Act*
http://tinyurl.com/c8u42q6

History of Banking: *An Asian Perspective*
http://tinyurl.com/boeehjl

The People's Voice: *Former Arizona Sheriff Richard Mack*
http://tinyurl.com/d62fyg3

Asset Protection: *Pure Trust Organizations*
http://tinyurl.com/btrjfqp

The Matrix As It Is: *A Different Point Of View*
http://tinyurl.com/ckrbkge

From Debt To Prosperity: *'Social Credit' Defined*
http://tinyurl.com/d2tjmw3

Give Yourself Credit: *Money Doesn't Grow On Trees*
http://tinyurl.com/d7tphuv

My Home Is My Castle: *Beware Of The Dog*
http://tinyurl.com/bmzxc2n

Commercial Redemption: *The Hidden Truth*
http://tinyurl.com/d9etg7w

Hardcore Redemption-In-Law: *Commercial Freedom And Release*
http://tinyurl.com/cl65vrz

Oil Beneath Our Feet: *America's Energy Non-Crisis*
http://tinyurl.com/btlzqxf

Untold History Of America: *Let The Truth Be Told*
http://tinyurl.com/bu9kjjc

Debtocracy: *& Odious Debt Explained*
http://tinyurl.com/cooqzuz

New Beginning Study Course: *Connect The Dots And See*
http://tinyurl.com/cxpk42p

Monitions of a Mountain Man: *Manna, Money, & Me*
http://tinyurl.com/cusgcqs

Maine Street Miracle: *Saving Yourself And America*
http://tinyurl.com/d4yktlw

Reclaim Your Sovereignty: *Take Back Your Christian Name*
http://tinyurl.com/cf5taxh

Gun Carry In The USA: Your Right To Self-defence
http://tinyurl.com/cdn3y3y

Climategate Debunked: *Big Brother, Main Stream Media*
http://tinyurl.com/d6gy2xz

Epistle to the Americans I: *What you don't
know about The Income Tax*
http://tinyurl.com/d99ujzm

Epistle to the Americans II: *What you don't
know about American History*
http://tinyurl.com/cnyghyz

Epistle to the Americans III: *What you don't
know about Money*
http://tinyurl.com/cp8nrh8